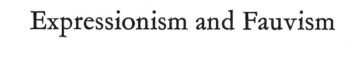

Expressionism and Fauvism

The Revolution in Printmaking
from Romanticism to the Present

Edited by Walter Koschatzky
Director of the Graphic Collection of the Albertina

Kristian Sotriffer

EXPRESSIONISM AND FAUVISM

McGraw-Hill Book Company
New York · Toronto

Picture Credits

The Albertina, Vienna (Photo Lünemann): color plates I, III, IV, V, VI, X, reproductions 1, 7, 9–18, on pages 51, 61, 63, 71, 73, reproductions 18–27, 32, 34–37, 40, 42. — Author's collection: reproductions on pages 13, 30, 53, 72, 95, 97, 99, 109, 111, and illustrations numbered 2, 3, 5, 6, 8, 33, 38, 39, 41, 43–50. — Dresden collection of copper engravings: illustration number 31. — Günther Franke, Munich: reproduction on page 103, and illustration number 28. — Folkwang Museum, Essen (Photo C. and H. Milch): color plates VII and IX. — Munch Museum, Oslo: color plate II, illustration number 4. — The Museum of Modern Art, New York: illustration number 30. — Philadelphia Museum of Art (Photo A. J. Wyatt): illustration number 29. — Städtische Galerie, Munich: color plate VIII

Translated from the German
Expressionismus und Fauvismus
by Richard Rickett, Vienna
German edition © 1972 by Anton Schroll & Co., Vienna
This edition © 1972 by Anton Schroll & Co., Vienna
Library of Congress Catalog Card Number 72-1576
SBN 07-059 764-2
Printed in Austria and Switzerland

Expressionism and Fauvism

All art may be described as the *expression,* in a formal medium, of sensations, observations, and visualized thoughts – the more or less extreme compression of experience into the subjective mode. Hence if a style is to be entitled "Expressionism," it needs special standards by which it may be distinguished from other accepted forms of artistic expression, and it must be defined.

The style or concept of "Expressionism" was confronted by an established approach to human reality that was largely a survival of the artistic thinking of the nineteenth century and the "art nouveau" that grew out of it. Its development produced controversial attempts to define the boundaries of the new movement. As the phenomenon "Expressionism" recedes into the past, it becomes possible to clarify its specific characteristics, although it remains as hard as ever to fix its boundaries or to confine oneself to a description of "classical Expressionism."

An understanding of what essentially constitutes Expressionism perhaps can be facilitated by considering it as a "manner" rather than a "style." Its underlying characteristic (and this includes literary and musical Expressionism) consists of an over-intensification of experience, a rejection of the classical canon, a distortion and exaggeration bordering on the hysterical, a shattering of traditional forms and the reordering of the fragments to make vehicles for changed thinking and sensation, and a new, more critical and emphatic approach to the world. In its origins, admittedly, it must be regarded as an intellectual compulsion to break with tradition. If we are to call any particular, well-marked form of life and thought a "style," then its reflection in art as such must be recognizable. In the present case a particular form of artistic expression was adopted as a goal; its motivation as well as its practical and theoretical foundations were consciously recognized, and this led to the development of a style that became independent of the mere fact of expression. This was "Expressionism," but the exact delimitation of the concept still remained unfixed. Even before the term had been coined the roots of its unrestricted possibilities may be discerned, for instance, in the work of the great trio Gauguin, Van Gogh, and Munch – a matter to which we shall return later.

In the course of the development of Expressionism, from the turn of the century up to the various forms in which it was carried on – whether diluted or with a shift of emphasis, or with changed significance as after the First World War – contemporaries produced a wide variety of impressions and definitions of it. In any case Expressionism only crystallized in a pure and unmistakable form in Germany – more precisely in central and south Germany – and even there was often enough subject to influences of Romanticism and Symbolism, and of a mystic approach peculiar to itself, so that it came to expression differently and in constrasting forms in the works of the various conspicuous artists.

Expressionism arose from a feeling of crisis and a loss of identity; it heralds the beginning of the end of the bourgeois world. The following specimen of the emphatic manner peculiar to the Expressionists comes from Hermann Bahr: "Never was an epoch so shaken by horror and the dread of death. Never was the world so plunged in the silence of the grave. Never was man so small. Never was he so afraid. Never was joy so distant and freedom so dead. Now distress cries out: man cries out for his soul; the whole epoch becomes one cry of distress. Art joins in the cry: it cries into the black depths, cries for help, cries for spirit: *that is Expressionism.*"

Others adopted a more critical attitude towards the phenomenon, more particularly when they had learned to see it in better perspective. Carl Einstein described "Expressionism" as "a cheap, empty word," Kasimir Edschmid as "a catchword of uncertain scope," but the latter did recognize in the Expressionist approach the wish to see "existence as a great vision":

"Thus the whole of space becomes vision for the Expressionist artist. He doesn't see, he looks. He doesn't describe, he experiences. He doesn't reproduce, he forms. He doesn't take, he seeks. Now we no longer have the concatenation of facts: factories, houses, illness, whores, outcry and hunger. Now we have the vision of them. Facts have significance only so far as the artist's hand, reaching through them, grasps at what lies behind. Art, which seeks only the essentials, excludes the incidental.... A profile is hammered out for the whole, giving it line and ordered form."

Expressionism has revolution in mind, and the conquest of new ideas, changing the social pattern. Hence even Nature was torn apart "from top to bottom" (W. Michel) for the Expressionist. The outer appearances of the world were no longer self-evident: now they were challenges to transformation, to reinterpretation on the basis of ecstatic discharges of emotion, seldom backed by a theoretical framework, but originating, rather, in the subjective, program-directed will.

The Expressionist tended to lose himself in an emotional ejaculation couched in superlatives, a fact which later drew from Jean Bazaine the comment that the Expressionist was no revolutionary, "but only a rebel, who wants to avenge himself on a world which he actually sees as unalterable." Whatever one may think of that aspect of the matter, it must be admitted that the achievements of Expressionist artists, whether pioneering in development from the existing or in reaction to it, provided the basis for the more recent developments in art. Their efforts, when adapted to other purposes, formed the foundation for a large number of the artistic theories adopted in the twentieth

6

century; one of these is "Abstract Expressionism," as developed after the Second World War. Cubism and Surrealism derived from endeavors of a similar nature.

In the course of two years the French developed a forcible, new, post-Impressionist view of the world, related to Expressionism; but in contrast to the Germans they did not break with tradition, or when they did, then only partially. Expressionism, for Matisse, lay "in the overall arrangement of the picture. Composition is the art of arranging, in a decorative manner, the various elements of which the painter disposes for the expression of his feelings." What had been called "Fauvism" – the art of "fierce animals" – culminated in an exhibition at the Paris Salon d'Automne in 1905, almost at the same time as the founding of the Dresden art group "Die Brücke" (The Bridge). Van Gogh and Gauguin, whose works were represented in big exhibitions in 1901 and 1903, were among the forerunners of this group, which at the start included, above all, Matisse, Rouault, Vlaminck, and Derain, and which was joined in 1906 by Braque and Dufy. But in contrast to the majority of the Germans, the French concentrated on color, with the result that for them the art of prints and drawings could never achieve the representative significance that it had for the Expressionists. The role of the woodblock-cutter's knife (the ferocious use of which undoubtedly reflected the psychological state of the user) was played mainly by color as in the case of Vlaminck, for instance, who spoke of blowing the State Art Gallery to pieces with cobalt and vermilion. Derain compared color to charges of dynamite. But Fauvism was hardly more than an episode, and when Matisse opened his own school of painting in Paris in 1907, and Cézanne, after a big exhibition, became known to the initiators of Cubism, such as Braque, the French appeared to have already forgotten that which was just energetically starting to assert itself in Germany, namely a form of expression that is direct, instinct based, and fundamentally unmethodical; that, in Vlaminck's words, seeks human, not artistic truth.

Prints

An artistic impulse that aimed at representing the contrasts and the drama of the world, at recording an age of machines, cities, and dynamic movements which were threatening to crush humanity rather than liberate it, was dependent on suitable media. The idiom of Expressionism in its best days is of a lapidary, token-like nature, simplifying although by no means simple; the object to be represented is reduced to significant planes and lines, so that it is grasped as a whole, not detail by detail. In painting, this procedure leads to a broad treatment that utilizes surfaces and unmixed colors in contrasting and complementary arrangements. But the desired simplification and lapidary effect could be achieved more powerfully and strikingly, optically more effectively, in prints, and above all, of course, in woodcuts. This last technique is certainly the most important for the Expressionists, the best suited to their purpose. Hence it produced the most engaging works, the most convincing and prima facie captivating. The Expressionists not only recalled the woodcut to life by being the first since the Middle Ages to rediscover and respect its peculiarities, they also raised it to an unexampled flowering. What lithography and etching, thanks to the fine nuances obtainable with them, were for the Impressionists, the woodcut, which the genius of Gauguin and Munch mastered from the start, was for the Expressionists. Etching and lithography, in comparison, play a subordinate role, although direct work on the metal plate with the dry point or on the stone with tusche produce effects that are quite adequate for the expressive requirements of the particular case. But the wood itself, quite naturally and directly, opened up for the artist the possibility of producing effects which could only be created in other materials as a result of considerable thought. Expressionism is a style based principally on contrast and surface as opposed to line. Prints and drawings, above all the former, provided an ideal means of realizing the conceptions of the artist striving for spontaneity. Consequently, nearly all the Expressionists made prints, and for some of them prints played a central role. Their painting style was not infrequently formed by that developed in the particular printmaking technique they favored.

I Vincent van Gogh: "Portrait of Dr. Gachet" ("L'homme à la pipe"). Etching. 1890. 181 x 150 mm. Signed in the top righthand corner 15 (25?) Mai 90. Original dimensions.
This is Van Gogh's only etching, and the material for it was provided by Dr. Gachet himself. It may well rank as one of the incunabula among Expressionistic etchings. The mobility in the delineation of the facial features is more pronounced than in most portraits. The etching was completed about two months before Van Gogh's death at Auvers-sur-Oise.

I VAN GOGH

The changed world picture

Around 1900 the intellectual world began to change. Many artists, already tentatively feeling their way into the new century, and at the same time far more deeply rooted in the old than most of the revolutionary innovators realized, experienced the necessity of finding something new on which to base their work. The concept of reality had changed for them; they, no less than the natural scientists, saw humanity in a new light. They understood that, as Franz Marc put it, "art is concerned with the profoundest things, that its renovation must not be confined to form, but must be a rebirth of thinking."

They experienced the spiritual totality of the world afresh, in its excerpts no less than in the whole; they attempted to grasp the inner unity of nature, not its objective appearances. Even though (at least until the emergence of Kandinsky) German Expressionism attempted to articulate its new experience on the basis of individual appearances, its endeavors were profoundly rooted in Romantic ideas of seeking the wholeness of the world; the French on the other hand (the short Fauvist period apart) operated as analysts and synthesists (thus producing Cubism), the Italians as anarchical Futurists.

All these tendencies – related to one another by the fact that they seek and occupy new positions, and that they no longer portray, but take part – have this in common: they seek in art the possibility of effecting more, of expressing more, rather than merely clothing in a beautiful garment what the retina is capable of taking in. The Expressionists did not see only with their eyes; they saw mainly from within, outwards. Wilhelm Burger, writing as a contemporary and companion in arms, puts it as follows: "Art still endeavours, as it always has, to communicate a content that makes the elemental world of creative thought into an immediate, perceptual experience. The subtle riches of sensory experience are no more in place in this art than is the artistic skill of the virtuoso; but the inventive richness of artistic imagination, and the expressive power of its individual, perceptual unity are all the more important. In the presentment of the unifying primal essence of things this 'new art' transcends the oppositions of this world and the other world, of man and nature, of man and beast, or of the sexes."

In their determination to find a new orientation, artists around 1900 searched in practically every quarter. The experience of early medieval woodcuts, of the art of strange peoples preserved in ethnological collections and of folk art – all these came together in their thinking and their work. Symbolical and mystical ideas, such as were developed from Blake to Redon and carried forward, unquestioned, by Gauguin and Munch, together with the Romantics' cosmic feeling of the Infinite, brought to expression in the Art Nouveau style, were the points from which Expressionism developed or departed. A new religious feeling, as well as the revolt against established bourgeois life-patterns, with the attendant criticism of social conditions, formed a further admixture. The longing to break out into unknown regions, the tendency towards world renunciation and asceticism, the thought of death all formed their minds no less than did their passionately exaggerated behavior and their rejection of standards which they had learned to see as hollow. Thus Expressionism is characterized by an ecstatic urge to break out of a mental and physical prison. The painters and draftsmen fought alongside writers, musicians, and increasingly critical-minded political people in their demand for a "new society." The final outcome, and the reasons why the striving of the Expressionists was doomed to failure in the end, are perhaps of little consequence when compared with the artistic achievements they left behind them, but they also will be considered later.

The Expressionist artist, grown receptive to all phenomena that appeared, in their spontaneity and genuineness, to correspond to his aims, threw himself open to everything that had not hitherto been considered worthy of attention, or at least of public attention. It was not by chance that in 1913 Giovanni Papini described the five types of creative man as the savage, the child, the lunatic, the criminal, and the genius. In these the possibility was seen of realizing potentialities as human beings unhampered by the restraints of civilization. The statements of artists concerning their relationship to the self-expression of children, so-called primitives, and the mentally deranged begin with Gauguin. Van Gogh maintained that everything came from his "mad imagination," while Gauguin described himself as "something that is incapable of being ridiculous: a child and a savage." Derain told Vlaminck that it was necessary to be eternally young, eternally a child: "One could make beautiful things all through one's life. On the other hand if one becomes civilized one turns into a machine for optimum adaptation to life, and nothing more!"

"The present day," Burger said, "sees a lost paradise in the enigmatical unity of nature and man in the 'primitive,' in the unconcealed richness of his inner life; and even the proud forebears of our own European culture lose the nimbus of aristocratic singularity as soon as their oriental roots are known."

In the retrospect of his book *Barbaren und Klassiker*, which appeared in 1922, Wilhelm Hausenstein gives the following definition, which originated in the spirit of the Expressionist epoch, although he subsequently changed his views: "Illiteracy is the essence of art. People who can read do not create shapes, they write the alphabet; they do not build houses, but let advertisements

Maurice de Vlaminck: *Girl's head*. Woodcut, about 1905.
101 x 159 mm.

and frontages run riot; . . . it follows that among savages who are still worthy of the name, art is not confined to a professional class which is a kind of lateral excrescence, and which one might call the artistry."

The principles of bourgeois aesthetics were laid open to controversy by such identifications as these, and through the mediacy of art-psychology they were increasingly superseded by the definition of the artistic phenomenon given by Max Verworn in a lecture on the psychology of primitive art at Cologne in 1907, namely "a means of expression adopted by man for sensations and conceptions, thoughts and feelings." Once such a theory as this is accepted, it naturally becomes impossible to discriminate any longer between so-called fine art and the productions of the artistically untrained. This theme is still a subject for discussion, and at the present time, when the art theories held by the Expressionists have long been superseded by others, it is of particular interest. It should not, however, be overlooked that the years around 1900 were the starting point for all those theories that have subjected art to a state of permanent revolution. "As man changes, so do his forms," as August Macke assserted in *Der Blaue Reiter*. In a letter to him written in 1911, after a visit to the Ethnological Museum, Franz Marc had emphasized the unquestioned fact that "it is in this cold first dawn of artistic intelligence that we seek the rebirth of our artistic feelings, not in cultures with a thousand years behind them, like the Japanese or the Italian Renaissance."

Themes, Models, and Motivations

The world of objects that stimulates the artist changes together with his orientation in the world of ideas; his field of vision narrows or widens in proportion to the motivation to undertake the labor of creation. There are typical "subjects" to which the artist turns, which answer his desire to draw forms from within himself, to find an echo in the outer world to the forces working in him. For this purpose he is led to treat forms "according to his requirements," as Kandinsky put it. A congruity arises between content and form, between the need of expression and its counterpart in the subjective formulation of that which is seen or experienced; this applies not only in painting, but naturally also in prints. The models for woodcuts, etchings, and lithographs were often artistic solutions already embodied in paintings, and conversely representations first realized in prints were transferred, by the use of different means, to canvas. Examples of this are frequent primarily among the members of the "Brücke" group.

The work of the great majority of Expressionist and post-Expressionist artists was determined by three major categories of subject. First, the War, foreseen and by some longed for, which brought Expressionism, as an innovating movement, to a sudden end; secondly, the love of great cities, shared by many painters and writers; and finally, in connection with such themes as these, a revolutionary element: the belief in a possible upheaval as such. In those of a sensitive and romantic turn of mind, more closely bound to Nature, we also find a feeling of interrelationship with the Cosmos, as with Franz Marc, for whom the animal was the bearer of "inner mystic construction," or Kandinsky, who said of his own work, partly Expressionist in feeling as it was, that technically "it arose like the Cosmos, through catastrophes which end by creating a symphony, called the music of the spheres, out of the chaotic blaring of the instruments. The creation of works is the creation of the world."

It is impossible to find a common denominator for all the endeavors of the Expressionists; we find among them the most divergent tendencies such as are represented, with intent, in the illustrations in this volume. But the premonition of an imminent catastrophe and an upheaval not solely brought about by the War determined the formal perception, and the choice of a particular type of theme calculated to express it, in virtually all of them. If individual factors are discounted, their idiom is found to agree closely among themselves: a new concept of existence governs the rhythm and the interrelation of forms in their works. If Marc tries to "participate pantheistically in the quivering and coursing of blood in Nature, in the trees, in the beasts, in the air," and makes it into a picture with "new movements and with shadows," so do others attempt to participate in "the great human orchestra" which Max Beckmann felt the city to be.

"Let me paint what is near at hand," Ludwig Meidner demanded in 1914; "our urban world! The tumultuous streets, the elegance of iron suspension-bridges, the gasometers . . . the strident colour-schemes of buses and express engines, the waves of telephone-wires . . ." That could have been written by one of the Italian Futurists, whose joy in the representation of movement, of dramatic, dynamic incident that broke up the rectangular pattern of vertical and horizontal, was shared by many German Expressionists.

14

In 1919 Kurt Pinthus once again placed on record what "the stone-built city" meant to the Expressionist artist: "No longer the symbol of the ugly and inhuman, the refuge of poverty, but a counterpart to the open countryside: the work of our hands, the upraised temple of the community, in the tempestuous rhythm of which we are united."

For the town artists who identified themselves with their environment, the conflict between art and civilization did not exist as it did for those like Nolde and Pechstein, who followed in Gauguin's tracks to the South Seas or, like other painters of the "Brücke" group, sought the breath of Nature among the lakes and dunes of north Germany.

But the War and the latent unrest that preceded it, mounting to an agonizing intensity in the breasts of the artists, and compelling them to elemental renderings of their state of inner feeling, did not come to expression so much in what they portrayed as in the violence and explosive force of that which their passionate sympathy caused them literally to hurl at the world. Thus the Expressionist artists may be seen, without excess of irony, as "specialists in suffering," as Wolfgang Rothe saw them in his capacity, up to 1914, as a prophet of the War, and afterwards as its chronicler. "The 'brother-man' feeling of the Expressionist generation of artists," Rothe stated, "not only included the whore, the madman, and the criminal among those it embraced, it also raised these outlaws of bourgeois society, these outcasts, to the rank of artistic commonplaces."

The Expressionists were sympathizers, and they called others to sympathy. An attitude such as that which Paul Klee coolly recorded in his diary in 1914, namely that he had long had "this war" in him, so that "inwardly it was no concern of his," would have aroused the criticism of many of his contemporaries. The Expressionists regarded themselves, at least to a certain extent, as world improvers. As such they felt obliged to come forth from studios and "ivory towers" and to put the unity of art and life into practice – a feat in which, it must be admitted, very few were successful. Kurt Hiller (*Das Ziel*, 1916), an activist and one of the most violent critics of his Expressionist contemporaries, commented bitterly on their repeated failures in this respect: "One was nervy, complex, and sensitive – terribly sensitive – and the World War was allowed after all. (The guilt lay not with ministers, generals, or grand dukes, but with *l'art pour l'art*.)"

In summer 1918, Kurt Pinthus, then a soldier, composed a "Speech for the Future" (published in *Die Erhebung*, 1919). He recognized that art was "not flight from the reality of the spirit – not sedative but exciting (which does not mean that excitement is art). Therefore, definitions of art as 'noble simplicity and silent greatness,' or as 'disinterested satisfaction' are misleading and harmful. Art was never for art's sake, but for man's."

It was the War that first caused Max Beckmann to depart from a path that seemed to have predestined him for the career of a society painter. In Strasbourg, in 1915, he painted his self-portrait as a medical orderly, and this work marks his conversion to Expressionism. In April 1915 he wrote from the front: "I want to digest all this, so that afterwards I shall be quite free to make almost timeless things: this black human countenance, looking out from the grave, and the silent dead who approach me are dark salutations from eternity, and as such I want to paint them later."

One of the most gripping chroniclers of the War was Otto Dix, who made over six hundred drawings during its course, bringing formal elements from Fauvism and Cubism-Futurism together in one great outburst, working them up into a reeling, plunging, exploding "revolt of the German spirit against itself," as Jean Cassou remarked. Otto Conzelmann noted that Dix saw in the War "not only a consequence of the technology that man himself had created; he experienced it as a ruthless, unfeeling outburst of Nature, beyond good and evil: like a tidal wave or a typhoon – a shock that sent a shudder through the earth, down to its foundations." Dix's War drawings served as the basis for the fifty etchings of his War series, carried out in 1923 – 1924; these can be compared to "Los Desastres de la guerra" which Goya, the model and forerunner of all Expressionists, had etched more than a hundred years earlier.

The Models

The Expressionists had three great models, more recent than Goya, for the task they had set themselves, particularly in their prints – a task which demanded, first of all, that they should come to terms with the material with which they were dealing. These were: first, Van Gogh, who impressed by the sincerity and the power underlying his work; then, even more important, Gauguin and Munch, who may be regarded as the precursors of the Expressionists in the art of the woodcut. The stimulus they gave cannot be exaggerated, even if they were not responsible for every single technical innovation.

In any case it was they who in many respects inaugurated the Expressionist epoch, although they themselves were predominantly rooted in a Symbolistic attitude. Many influences can be traced: in France, Japanese colored woodcuts had been discovered, and these proved important above all for the Nabis, that artistic group in which at times Gauguin's influence had been paramount. Here the Expressionists' idea or theory of the community-forming power of art (to be carried further by the "Brücke" artists) was anticipated, as well as their striving to produce a unity of art and life. The Nabis, furthermore, were already modeling themselves on the art of the people, e. g., the Breton *calvaires* or the Epinal picture sheets, just as the group of friends centered in the "Blaue Reiter" were later to find inspiration in the Bavarian paintings on the underside of glass.

"I find the humblest woodcut, with its broad patches of colour, as admirable as a Rubens or a Vermeer," said Van Gogh, who had organized an exhibition of Japanese woodcuts in 1887.

To Gauguin he said: "Even if the Japanese are making no further progress in their own country, at least their art is undoubtedly continuing its development in France." After the famous Japanese exhibition at the Ecole des Beaux Arts in early autumn 1890, Gauguin came to be known as *"le Nabi très japonard."* It was then that Maurice Denis formulated the famous precept, so important for the creators of prints: *"Se rappeler qu'un tableau – avant d'être un cheval de bataille, une femme nue ou une quelconque anecdote – est essentiellement une surface plane recouverte de couleurs en un certain ordre assemblées."* (Remember that a painting – before being a war horse, a nude woman, or some anecdote or other – is essentially a surface plane covered with colors, assembled in a certain order.) Incidentally, the Arnold Gallery, subsequently of some importance for the "Brücke" painters, showed an exhibition of Japanese prints in Dresden as early as 1895. Munch, who was introduced to Japanese prints during his stay in Paris, fell under their influence just as Toulouse-Lautrec did. Both had their printing done at Clot and Lemercier's.

But it was Gauguin who first found the path that led away from the chasing work of the wood engravers to a free and sovereign approach to the woodcut. In 1901 he gave the following comment on this approach to Daniel de Monfreid: "It is precisely because this technique turns back to the primitive days of woodblock cutting that it is so interesting, particularly in view of the tendency of the woodcut illustration to turn ever more into wood-engraving illustration. . . . I am sure that my woodcuts, which differ so strongly from everything that is being produced in prints, will prove their value one day."

Gauguin, like Munch, used the raw wood of packing cases in order to allow his material, the structure and roughness of the wood itself, to come to expression, for he held fast to his perception of the fact that the essential was to proceed boldly, following up the original impetus. "Don't polish too much," he commanded; "the subsequent hunting out of endless refinements only impairs the

first draft; that is the way to let the incandescent lava grow cold, to petrify your foaming blood."
Practically all the Expressionists were later to adopt this precept.

Gauguin also frequently made use of blocks which he made up out of a number of small, hard beech stocks, cut at right angles to the grain. He fitted in the drawing with fine lines and hatching, and cut away whole areas with the knife. It was possible to make free variations in every hand impression of such stocks. After his second stay in Tahiti he cut in coarser, softer wood, seeking a way of enriching the two-color woodcut, for which purpose he continued to work on the block after the first printing, then made impressions on the thinnest Japanese paper, and pasted these over the first impressions. This technique produced chiaroscuro effects peculiar to itself.

Munch displayed a similar inventive and unorthodox tendency. His work was described by Carl Zigrosser as expressive rather than Expressionist, with the exception of many of his woodcuts. In 1895 he saw the woodcuts which Gauguin had brought from Tahiti in 1893. He had made his first experiments with prints – in dry point for a start – a year earlier in Berlin. Erich Bütner, a Berlin painter and graphic artist, describes Munch at work as follows:

"I visited the master-printer Dannenberger at Lassaly's, and saw how Munch's work was printed. I was not a little astonished to see the color-plates in woodcut in the form of pieces cut out with the saw and inked, some green, some red, after which the rectangle was fitted together like a child's puzzle and put through the press. This produced a print of several colors and continuous grain, all in one operation."

Munch enjoyed experimenting, and made numerous variants of his woodcuts; he also combined relief printing with lithography, as in "The Vampire" (Schiefler catalogue 34).

Gustav Schiefler, the first to take a serious interest in Munch's prints and the author of the first catalogue of his works, describes Munch's manner of working as follows: "Nobody has ever treated technique in such a cavalier fashion: he is best suited by the simplest tools and the most intractable material. That is why he has to aim at the most powerful effects. He really does take rough pine-wood slats from packing-cases, working on them with a coarse knife and utilizing the grain and the saw-marks as welcome texture of the background. No niggling forms of technique suit him; his tools have to be as simple and as big as his ideas."

Munch was forever on the lookout for simplifications, clarifications, and concentrations of his themes. He produced his famous woodcut "The Kiss" in four different states between 1897 and 1902. He, like Gauguin, had rediscovered the intrinsic values of the different media for print-

18

II EDVARD MUNCH

making, had experimented with them and drawn from them that vital force that has established him, up to the present day, as the much admired model for all print enthusiasts, whether themselves artists, amateurs, or collectors.

The visions and grotesque fantasies of many Expressionists were to some extent anticipated, and their further development influenced by James Ensor. His grimacing masks and demons, and the symbolical ground from which such an idiom springs, are recognizable later in Paul Klee's early work, and in even greater degree in that of Emil Nolde. Wilhelm Fraenger, comparing Beckmann and Ensor, discovered in them the same "inner nerve of psychic necessitation." With Beckmann, he maintained, it was a matter of "the complete unhinging of spatial statics," of a figural style "that depersonalizes the human form to the extent of empty phantomism, and of a kind of composition in which the various picture-factors accumulate to adventitious aggregates." He found that the form of these displayed the same elements as with Ensor.

The Essence of Expressionist Prints

Expressionist prints display a number of characteristics that are best explained in the light of opposing theories that were previously, as well as subsequently, held in this field.

The most striking feature is the abandonment of that classical, aesthetic, ordered framework that makes a print easily comprehensible from the start. The impetuous, sometimes violent quality of Expressionist prints finds its realization in a harsh manner that presupposes nothing and acknowledges no canon, accepting no conditions other than those imposed by material and surface, both of which demand an understanding and respect for their requirements. No attempt is made at illusionism or the rendering of mass: the only thing that counts is the self-contained quality of the print, which must assimilate and subordinate to itself all the perceptual and sensory material to be rendered. Perfection in the ordering of line or surface is not sought; it may take form in the course of the work, but is sometimes deliberately destroyed again in order that nothing merely decorative, nothing solely aesthetic and therefore lacking binding relevance should take form. In place of cunningly contrived compositions we find spontaneity; technical refinements and artificial tricks give way to crude penetrations – with no attempt at perfection – into the substance. Between the material and the artist a dialogue arises, the latter communicating the violence of his feelings without much constraint.

The revulsion from merely "beautiful" prints, suitable for charming decoration, admittedly goes farther back: it is no exclusive discovery of the Expressionists', although the latter, in contrast to the French, are distinguished by the absolute subjectivity of this process. Camille Pissarro, in a letter, urges his son Lucien to be careful not to allow his woodcuts to sink to the category of arts and crafts, or of commercial goods. He advises him to make do without refinements, since these are incompatible with the matter in hand, and his ideas in some respects anticipate what was to become the goal of the Expressionists:

"In short, follow up your earlier works. In this the kind of cut is of great importance. Don't make your task more difficult than it need be, and don't take excessive pains with the perfection of the printing. What I'm afraid of is that with this confounded aestheticism you'll be turning out nothing but what's pretty. And in fact what matters is just the opposite. All the products of the official schools 'draw pretty-pretty,' and either they're very mannered or else they become unbalanced and clumsy. You must jealously guard that precious harshness that gives your early works the stimulating quality that commends them to all connoisseurs."

In the works of Munch and Gauguin, Pissarro's demands, and even the more extreme ones made by the Expressionists, are at least partly fulfilled. It is true that the linear elegance of Art Nouveau is to some extent still perceptible in the early works of the "Brücke" artists, particularly in Kirchner, and above all in the "Blaue Reiter" group; but the ideal Expressionist technique in prints is direct, vehement, rich in awareness and invention, born of curiosity and the joy of attack. There is pleasure, too, in wounding the block or plate before the artist. The product of this collision and interaction of artist and material does not acquire its aesthetic and its fascination from some conception of beauty communicated to block or plate; rather does it develop them independently of the representation, out of itself. But these products were not at once recognized for what they were, suffering virulent attack from contemporaries accustomed to the finely stylized but long perverted products of the nineteenth century in this field. The artist's thought, unruly but guided by a definite goal, had to accommodate itself to the material he had chosen and from which he worked.

Nevertheless, the impression given by Expressionist prints may be various, and can be mixed. Where no attempt was made to achieve perfection in the academic sense, it was not always possible to achieve the perfection of the imperfect as it appears in the best works, for example, E. L. Kirchner. In the last resort even the Expressionists could not always free themselves of a factor that menaces every artist, namely routine.

22

Gustav Hartlaub, who dealt in detail with the new valuation of the art of printmaking which the Expressionists enforced, described their work in this field as a confession of faith and as "unconditional utterance." It was no longer "an art for lovers of transpositions by pettifogging specialists, or of technical refinements and curiosities, and therefore it demanded a different attitude in the collector. The new type of collector had to go unhesitatingly for artistic content rather than rarity and all the varieties of 'collectors' value.' Of course the value of a print was still affected by the quality of the printing – in an etching by the particular 'state,' in a lithograph by the quality and the coloration – and in raised-field prints the introduction of 'hand-impression' and hand-colored copies have brought with them yet further points of discrimination against the prints of the standard edition. But such differences as these should henceforth only be judged from the point of view of the heightening of the artistic pleasure which a good copy, as compared to an inferior one, gives its owner; they must be judged only as the artist himself would judge them in the process of creation if he had personally supervised every impression – as he might have wished to do, in the interests of a full 'realization.' Early impressions and unique exemplars were no longer assembled in a non-artistic, sporting spirit, or for scholarly – or even commercial – purposes. Print-collecting could no longer be centered round the cabinet of the private capitalist, for prints had become more a matter for the public, for the people. Graphic art, above all in the form in which it had become so important, namely the woodcut, refused to stay put in portfolios – it wanted to fly, to flutter down from spiritual clouds into the outstretched hands of a wide public . . . ."

In a letter to August Macke of 12 June 1914, Franz Marc sought to bring out the difference between the points of departure of the Germans and the French: "What has the *peinture* of the Orphists got to do with me? No, we can't ever do such beautiful work as the French – or at least the Latins. We Germans are and always will be the born print-makers; we are still illustrators even when we paint."

Interesting though it may be, this statement needs correction, for the Orphists (Delaunay) exerted an undisputed influence on German artists, and on Marc and the "Blaue Reiter" group in particular. But when Marc says "We can't ever do such beautiful work as the French," he is right insofar as the latter's love of order and pronounced tendency to objectivity is in fact an essential distinguishing mark as contrasted with the subjective pathos of the Germans. Matisse may serve as an example that stands for others: he is concerned in his prints and drawings, even in his Fauve period, with closed form, and with line that communicates space. It is true that in the period around 1906, when

III Ernst Ludwig Kirchner: "Hungarian dance." Lithograph in three colors from three stones on yellow paper. 1909. 330 x 380 mm. Dube 123.
With his usual lightness of touch Kirchner uses a granulated surface for his stenographic treatment of this scene in order to bring out its essential movement. At this period of his career Kirchner had a particular partiality for scenes from circus life – dancers, riders, etc.

IV Max Pechstein: "Acrobats I." Woodcut, colored by hand. 1912. 270 x 200 mm. Fechter 87. Original dimensions.
At the time Pechstein completed this woodcut he had not yet experienced the artistic stimulus of his voyage to the Palau (Pelew) Islands, though the influence of exotic art is already apparent. There are ten extant copies of this woodcut.

he was making his lithographs and linocuts of figures and women's heads, his art was shaped by a certain vehemence, but this comes nowhere near the deformations with which the "Brücke" artists were attempting, at the same time, to set up a new basis on which they could learn to give articulate form to their encounter with another world.

For Carl Zigrosser the earliest manifestation of Expressionism as such reaches maturity with the "Brücke" artists. They were certainly the ones who showed the greatest consistency and independence in their innovations, and who for years exerted the most lasting effect on the artistic scene of their times. Nolde's confession of faith regarding his work applied to all of them: "I am so anxious for my work to grow out of my material. There are no such things as fixed rules of aesthetics. The artist creates the work in accordance with his nature and his instinct."

The art of Expressionist prints lives by contrasts, and it is clear that the Expressionists found the woodcut the ideal simplifying medium for bringing out opposites. In a letter to his cousin in 1919, Ernst Barlach wrote: "This technique is a challenge to a confession of faith and to the unmistakable presentation of what one really means. It enforces a certain generalized mode of expression, rejecting the unimportant effects produced by other processes that are less laborious, or more concerned to please. I have completed a number of large woodcuts, all concerned with the distressing state of the times."

But the "Brücke" artists did not neglect other techniques, all of which they mastered in the course of time, learning from one another. Max Pechstein wrote: "In etching one can utilize the various technical tricks in endless exciting ways. One can coax silvery tones with the file, can clear away the mordant with the brush, or plough the tough needle, the instrument of the will, through the metal of the plate. What a variety of effects can be achieved in the lithograph, if one prepares the stone oneself, etches and prints oneself. That is the thing – one must do one's own printing! Making the ink more or less tacky, using the paper more or less damp, all give new charms and stimuli."

24

III   ERNST LUDWIG KIRCHNER

"In modern figure drawing the surfaces are rendered in brief outline," Kasimir Edschmid said in 1917 in a lecture on Expressionism, for which he claimed a varied ancestry "in accordance with the totality that underlies its ruling idea, everywhere, at all times . . . ." Creases, he said, are smoothed over; only the essential is modeled. "But the figure becomes the type . . . all incidentals are eliminated. The most important element determines the idea: we no longer have a thinker: no, thought itself; no longer a couple embracing: no, embrace itself." Munch had already seen the mattter in this light in 1895, in his "The Kiss" (Schiefler catalogue 22).

The great achievements of the graphic art of the Expressionists are of course anything but "illustration," as Marc maintained, but rather symbolical, visionary, elemental creation, the expression of a feeling for the totality of the world in contrast to the particularizing vision of the Impressionists – although in its beginnings Expressionism owed something to the Impressionists' simplified view of things and their disregard for perspective.

Lastly, a feature that is displayed particularly clearly in the Expressionist prints is the trend towards the fantastic and grotesque, representing the entry into a dream world – the figures of which, it is true, were not making their first appearance at this time, after the close of the nineteenth century. They are particularly characteristic of northern artists and play a leading role in the work of James Ensor. Alfred Kubin recorded his visions in prints as early as 1900; these were particularly impressive, and had a strong influence on Paul Klee. Edvard Munch and Emil Nolde were also in search of this demoniac element. The dream visions of the Ensors and Kubins led on to Surrealism, and a number of graphic artists in the present century have repeatedly brought their feeling for a threatened world to expression in the form of grotesquely deformed stylistic elements. In this they have followed a trend that reaches from Bosch, by way of Callot and Goya, to Arnulf Rainer, an artist falling essentially into the sphere of Expressionism, whose expeditions into the unconscious depths are characteristic.

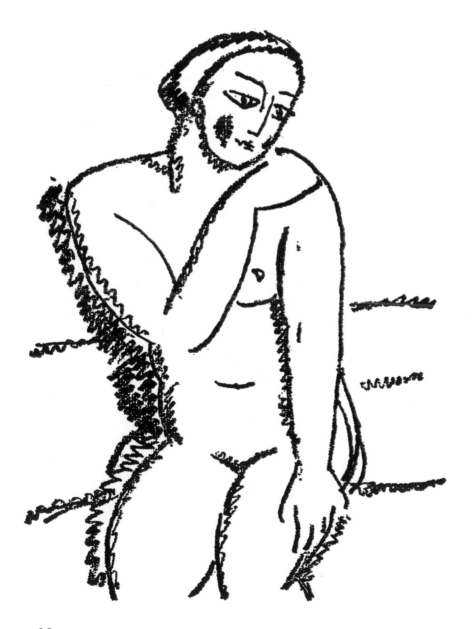

Alexei von Jawlensky: *Seated nude.*
Lithograph from the
"female nudes" series of 1912.

30

1 PAUL GAUGUIN, *Woman under a tree*. Woodcut. About 1900. 135 x 223 mm. Sykorowá 10. Reproduced original size.

Two proofs and four prints of the final state exist. This is the classical example of a woodcut along the grain on the simplest, only rough-planed, wood, the structure of which vitalizes the linear and expressive representation. A hand-printed copy, as is shown by the margins and the grain.

2 PAUL KLEE, *Meeting between two men, each crediting the other with superior status*. Etching on zinc. 1903. 118 x 226 mm. Kornfeld 7. Reproduced original size.

In the series of etchings executed between 1903 and 1905 Klee is seeking symbolic representation but at the same time anticipating certain aspects of Expressionism. Goya impressed him deeply at this time. "The etchings are the most immediate expression of his view of the world at that time" (Grohmann).

3 JAMES ENSOR, *Christ in agony*. Etching and dry-point on copper. 1895. 178 x 242 mm. Croquez 94. From 1885 onwards Ensor's work is interspersed with scenes from the life of Christ and other religious themes, which were to make a deep impression particularly on Emil Nolde, who met Ensor in 1911. One of Ensor's biographers writes: "No other means of expression could have enabled him to pore over life with the same over-fine intensity, or in the same silence, as the etching needle did."

4 EDVARD MUNCH, *Beach landscape (with washerwoman)*. Woodcut. 1903. 330 x 460 mm. Schiefler 210.

The shallow gouging, and the structures resulting from it in this hand-print, creates a certain restlessness which is however restored to orderliness by surface accents. The rendering of the interrelation of the human figure and the surrounding scenery is typical.

5 MAURICE DE VLAMINCK, *The Bridge in Chatou*. Woodcut. About 1914. 256 x 336 mm.

The influence of Van Gogh and the turbulence that comes to expression in his paintings appears reactivated in this classic example of a later Fauvist woodcut. Vlaminck "had no received ideas," as he himself said. "To be a painter is no more a profession than to be an anarchist, a lover, a runner, a dreamer or a boxer. It's an accident of nature."

6 GEORGES BRAQUE, *Nude*. Dry-point etching. 1908. 275 x 195 mm. Hoffmann 1.

Braque's first etching, in which "Cubism, Fauvism, and Expressionism" meet (Seuphor).

7 EGON SCHIELE, *Crouching woman*. Dry-point etching. 1914. 483 x 322 mm. Kallir 6 b.

In his graphic rendering of a body Schiele alternates between flowing lines and their interruption by angular, ordering strokes. He takes a kind of middle position between the semi-Cubist forms of Braque and the flowing lines of Matisse.

8 HENRI MATISSE, *Nude with footstool*. Lithograph. 1906. 415 x 195 mm. Catalog H. M., Bibliothèque Nationale, Paris (1970) 23.

With a free, simplifying movement the artist outlines his form in the manner of a gesture, in contrast to the swelling, classical lines of later variations on the same theme. Matisse produced his first lithographs in 1906 – a total of twelve women's heads and figures in Fauvist style. His very first prints were made on copper in 1903, when he was thirty-three. "Only those are artists," he said, "who are capable of subjecting their impressions to method and order."

9 RAOUL DUFY, *Bather*. Lithograph. 1918. 520 x 360 mm.

Dufy's later characteristic style is anticipated here, but is still dominated by dynamic, Expressionist features.

10 CHARLES GEORGE DUFRESNE, *Under palm-trees*. Etching. About 1920. 213 x 282 mm.
Dufresne began his career as a Naturalist, and was later the first to make a synthesis of the Fauvist and Cubist means of expression. He produced numerous etchings.

11 ERICH HECKEL, *Lake in a park. 1914*. Combination of dry-point etching and burin. 248 x 199 mm. Dube 122. Reproduced original size.
When Expressionists turned to etching they preferred the dry point, which gave them direct and controlled engraving straight on the plate and, like the woodcut, compelled them to reach definite formulations. This print was made for the Berlin publishers J. B. Neumann.

12 ERNST LUDWIG KIRCHNER, *Gewecke and Erna*. Dry-point on zinc. 1913. 250 x 208 mm. Dube 169. Reproduced original size.
The depth with which the steel cuts into the soft material gives a soft, velvety quality to the outlines in the print, thus moderating the austerity of the composition.

13 ANDRE DERAIN, *Four women bathing*. Copper engraving. About 1913. 176 x 198 mm. Reproduced approximately original size.
Cézanne, synthetic Cubism, and Expressionist forms are combined here, as in Dufresne, in a theme which is characteristic of this time. It expresses the rhythmical participation of human figures in a landscape. Nudes in a landscape constituted a central theme with both Fauvists and Expressionists.

14 WILHELM LEHMBRUCK, *Melancholy figures*. Dry-point etching. 1912. 200 x 245 mm. Petermann 37. Reproduced approximately original size.
Lehmbruck's graphic work is closely related to his sculpture, to which it forms the accompaniment from 1910 to 1919. "Hardly anywhere is there less thought of publication, printing, or turning to profit than in these works" (Petermann).

15 ERICH HECKEL, *Two wounded soldiers*. Woodcut. 1914. 421 x 272 mm. Dube 276/II.
In its lapidary expressiveness this is one of the most striking of the woodcuts based on Heckel's war experiences in Flanders. It was printed for the folio "Elf Holzschnitte, 1912–1919," published in 1921 by J. B. Neumann, Berlin. Heckel produced a total of 1,017 prints.

16 ERNST LUDWIG KIRCHNER, *Box at the theatre*. Woodcut. 1909. 195 x 318 mm. Dube 148.
The classic example of surface-cutting, the knife following the structure of the wood with virtuoso-like brilliance. According to Schiefler only three copies are in existence. The present reproduction was made from the Albertina copy.

17 EMIL NOLDE, *River-port*. Etching. 1910. 312 x 410 mm. Second state. Schiefler (1966) 144.
In Nolde's prints the qualities of painting predominate; even his woodcuts avoid sharp outlines, allowing forms to run over. And he was an etcher before he turned his attention, under the influence of the "Brücke" group, to woodcuts. As an etcher he preferred a richly-graded chiaroscuro. In his early days he had already copied Goya prints for their balanced combination of light and dark passages. "My etchings are not built up on thinking," he said, "they arise. It's true I do think a lot, but the moments in which I'm really creating are pure – free of everything that isn't art."

1 PAUL GAUGUIN

3 JAMES ENSOR

4 EDVARD MUNCH   5 MAURICE DE VLAMINCK

6 GEORGES BRAQUE

7 EGON SCHIELE   8 HENRI MATISSE

9 RAOUL DUFY

10 CHARLES GEORGE DUFRESNE
11 ERICH HECKEL
12 ERNST LUDWIG KIRCHNER

13 ANDRÉ DERAIN   14 WILHELM LEHMBRUCK

15 ERICH HECKEL   16 ERNST LUDWIG KIRCHNER

17 EMIL NOLDE

The "Brücke" as Example

The Expressionists, in their strongly pronounced community feeling, tended to form artists' groups and circles of friends, and of these the "Brücke" was not only the first but also the most important, from the point of view of both performance and influence. The members of this group were the earliest and probably the purest exponents of that agitated, concise style with its aims of simplification and forcefulness, which characterized the unmistakable artistic impulse, drawn from so many sources, that may be considered the essence of German Expressionism. This applies primarily to the work of Ernst Ludwig Kirchner, Erich Heckel, and Karl Schmidt-Rottluff. In collaboration these three did in fact work out their own style, distinct from that of contemporaries of Expressionist tendency but with different aims, in which, during the early period, when their association was closest, their separate individualities almost disappeared.

The young people who joined forces in Dresden in 1905 were by no means solely would-be or trained painters or graphic artists, but students of architecture whose preference, it is true, had always been for expression in pictorial form. They were Ernst Ludwig Kirchner and Fritz Bleyl, both 25, Erich Heckel, 22, and Karl Schmidt, 21, who subsequently called himself Schmidt-Rottluff, after his birthplace Rottluff in Saxony. It was he who proposed the formation of the group. Nolde, in Dresden from 1905 to 1907, was a member for a year, and to him Schmidt-Rottluff wrote that the "Brücke" wished "to attract all revolutionary elements and everything that is in a ferment." But in the words of Heckel, who met Schmidt-Rottluff as early as 1901, but Kirchner not until 1904: "Where we wanted to get to we didn't yet know." Kirchner's contributions were the most lively and impulsive. As early as 1898, in Nuremberg, he had already discovered Dürer's woodcuts and the stimulating plasticity of early woodblocks, and in Dresden in 1902 he was fascinated by an exhibition of Japanese colored woodcuts. In the ethnographical department of the Dresden Ethnological Museum he found the carvings of the Pelew Islanders, by which Max Pechstein was so moved on his South Sea voyage in 1913–1914. Pechstein joined the "Brücke" in 1906. At that time Kirchner, in the name of all the members, issued a first program, which demanded "Freedom of action and life . . . in relation to highly respectable seniors." There were three transistory members, who had no influence on the group in its character of a community which sometimes hankered after the romantic dream of a medieval guild; these were the Swiss Cuno Amiet, the Finn Axel Gallén Kallela, and the Hamburger Fritz Nölken. The last member, the lyrical outsider Otto Mueller, did not join until 1910.

Erich Heckel described the approach of the nuclear group as follows: "We are interested in simple,

Max Pechstein: *Girls bathing I*. Woodcut. 1911, 400 x 320 mm. Fechter 52. Further woodcuts in this series appeared in 1912. The sparing use of the knife in certain areas is deliberate and enhances the interplay of light and shade.

obvious happenings, and we have always drawn human beings – unposed and without tracings.... The essential, for us, was free of pathos; pathos was always suspect." This unpretentious attitude of the "Brücke" artists was another point of contrast to the emotional, exclamatory manner of some of their contemporaries.

Empty shop premises served as refuge and studio for the artists. They equipped them with fittings that they made themselves, thus giving practical expression to their idea of regarding art and life as a unity, and of creating an environment hand in hand with the development of their painting. This aim betrays the latent influence of the Art Nouveau attitude, particularly in its English variant, which these artists, in the early period at any rate, could no more escape than they could the derivatives of Impressionism. But they soon began to build up their own reality, to transform the world of visually perceptible objects, and to find new formulae for it. Their study of nature did not prevent them getting on the track of the laws governing surface-bound art, and stressing that which they recognized as essential. They simplified their forms to the extent of self-sufficiency, in which process the technical limitations of the woodcut were no hindrance but the greatest help to them, as Kirchner pointed out.

The woodcut was the special favorite of the "Brücke" artists. They did learn the other print techniques, mostly from one another, and in many cases they transposed their pictorial ideas, first developed in drawings and paintings, into the medium of prints, often achieving in the process the best realization of their purposes; but the woodcut predominated. They learned etching in 1906 from Nolde, and Schmidt-Rottluff made their first lithographs. From 1906 onwards they issued annual portfolios of their original prints, generally consisting of a title page and three works by one or more members. These served to recruit nonproducing members, some of whom, such as Gustav Schiefler and Rosa Schapire, were to concern themselves intensively with the "Brücke" prints, and to produce the first catalogue of these works. Six such portfolios appeared, but the seventh fell victim to the internal dissensions which had already developed in 1912, and brought about the dissolution of the group in 1913.

This group of friends spent their summers either together by the Moritzburg Lakes near Dresden or in Dangast, or sometimes traveling. They exhibited constantly in Dresden, and from 1907 onwards in other towns as well. In 1908 Pechstein moved to Berlin, where in 1909, with other painters, he founded the New Secession, in the exhibitions of which the "Brücke" painters took part.

In the autumn of 1910 an exhibition at the Arnold Gallery in Dresden was accompanied by one of the most original catalogues ever produced by the Expressionists: it was illustrated with woodcuts based on the paintings exhibited, an artist generally illustrating the work of a friend. By then "Die Brücke" had found recognition, but the attitude of the *Kölner Zeitung* in connection with an exhibition at Tietz's in Düsseldorf in 1911 reveals the lack of understanding with which these artists had to contend at the time, and which was to have such serious consequences some twenty years later, when a so-called wholesome popular reaction was mobilized. The newspaper criticism ran: "The pictures . . . from the point of view of painting as such, are the end of all art, a gross abuse. . . . What these artists serve up to us exudes the poison of the darkest haunts of vice in any large town, revealing a mental condition on their part that can really only be understood as pathological."

In the same year Kirchner, Heckel, and Schmidt-Rottluff also moved to Berlin, but in 1913 disagreements about the "Brücke Chronik" written by Kirchner brought about the breakup of the association.

The Artists

The prints of almost all the members of the "Brücke" reached their highest development while the artists were still members of the group. Kirchner takes first place, with an œuvre of endless richness and unequaled quality, which not only typifies Expressionism as a whole but even transcends it both in significance and influence. He was magnificently successful in assimilating everything that affected him, from Indian painting (the Ajanta frescoes) to early medieval woodcuts and "primitive" art, taking in Van Gogh, Munch, Art Nouveau, and Matisse by the way. Donald E. Gordon's comments on Kirchner's painting apply equally to his graphic work: "It is fascinating to watch how Kirchner develops unusual pictorial methods in order to project his own existential consciousness into the object, or to attempt to feel his way into and express the essentially indescribable uniqueness of others."

Kirchner generally developed his pictorial ideas first in drawings and paintings, transposing them into printing techniques later. The high value he attached to these, and the degree to which he struggled with them are revealed by his numerous comments on the subject (see p. 121). Carl Einstein gave an exact definition of the power emanating from Kirchner's work: "Observe the construction of his figures in these prints. He does not portray a head or a body – it builds itself up

from the centripetal or centrifugal tendency of free touches. Here a comparison may be permitted with Van Gogh, who transformed Impressionist color-patch technique into the rendering of the figure in planes. Patches, line currents, surfaces, cut in black and white, that are purely invented, make up a powerful figure construction that is sometimes enveloped in vibrating nets. Impressionist surface analysis is suggested in construction. The figures grow out of the well-considered play of free plane construction with which the prints are filled."

The Romantic of the group was Erich Heckel, a sensitive, lyrical person of "Gothic" taste who, like Kirchner, had first come under the influence of Art Nouveau, then that of Munch and Gauguin. A certain fragility characterizes even his woodcuts, which he often pulls together with borderlines. The gripping, more ruthless character of Schmidt-Rottluff's contemporaneous prints is completely absent here, yet Heckel's are still typical Expressionist art, although their attraction lies above all in their restraint. Heckel checked after the first impressions, often restarting work on his engravings years afterwards, and printing them on a wide variety of papers. He took up etching in 1906, working exclusively in dry point, and the greater part of his lithographs were produced between 1907 and 1909. An essential feature of his work is the attempt to produce space effects by the relationships of planes. His colored woodcuts were often produced by sawing the block into pieces which were separately colored and then fitted together again for the single printing.

Schmidt-Rottluff's manner in woodcut tended to the monumental, using large surfaces and sometimes a heavy, angular idiom. Although he did not neglect other techniques, it was in woodcut that he produced his most characteristic work, and that which distinguished him from the others. His style crystallizes out around 1910, revealing the impression made on him by exotic carvings, and later Cubist influence as well, although he only used the latter to heighten the expressiveness of his prints, which are barbarous in comparison with those of Kirchner and Heckel. Like these two he also made wood carvings; in fact, the action of cutting wood was not restricted to the low relief required in printing blocks.

Emil Nolde also tried all the processes, starting with etching in 1904 and going on to woodcuts in 1906. He drew his lithographs on transfer paper. "He records his impressions like sketches with a wide, full brush and in broad, sometimes grotesque forms," Schiefler remarked in 1907. Nolde was the most painterly of the group: he was less concerned with precise contour and exactly defined form. His etchings emphasize tone values and he often bit so many states that the plate was completely destroyed. In his own words: "The etchings are full of life – an intoxication, a dancing, a swaying and surging of tone. They aren't the kind of art that can be leisurely enjoyed in an armchair: they demand that the spectator should join them in their wild leaping." And he goes on to put Expressionist perception into words (1906): "If I were to put the 'torn, misplaced' contours 'right' in the academic sense I should come nowhere near this effect. I sit and go on working on each plate until my perception is satisfied...." G. F. Hartlaub wrote of Nolde: "In his technique and perception it is as though the work of Goya were transposed to a northern climate – translated into unmistakable Saxon corporeality; he feels memories awaking on the unconscious and half-conscious planes, and releases himself from their oppression by using his heavy-handed peasant humour to transform the frightening, demoniac quality into burlesque."

Prints were a determining factor for Max Pechstein too. He loved "powerful cutting in wood, the vigorous scraping of the needle on metal, the gentle hiss of chalk on stone." But his adaptability prevented him from making original contributions to the same extent as his friends.

Otto Mueller, lastly, differed fundamentally not only from the other "Brücke" members but also from all the principal exponents of Expressionism in his soft, oversensitive temperament and his self-imposed limitation in themes. What he sought in graphic art was painter's effects; a trained lithographer, he made varied and inventive experiments. He succeeded in combining woodcut and lithography with the aid of the transfer process, transferring an impression from a woodcut onto the stone and then printing it as a lithograph. His "Gypsy Collection," printed as comparatively late as 1926–1927, is regarded as his principal work, but more interest attaches to his experiments in enriching the lithograph, after its printing by the craftsman, with additional effects. Like all true artists in prints, he was more interested in the individual copy, specially treated by one technique or another, than in the standard edition.

The "Brücke" had followers not only in Dresden, where Otto Lange, Conrad Felixmüller, and Wilhelm Rudolph deserve special mention, but its influence also spread to Berlin (César Klein, Max Kaus) and the West (Heinrich Nauen).

The "Blaue Reiter" and "Sturm" groups

The association of artists known as "Die Brücke" was the only compact group of German Expressionists which, at least at the start, professed a common aim. It comprised all the artists who were capable of giving prints an importance that was not overshadowed by painting. Yet for a time its influence was not very great: it had only its own resources to rely on, and in Munich, for instance, which was rapidly becoming a center of new movements of international scope, it was a long time before the group achieved any sort of recognition, and not a particularly enthusiastic one at that.

It was in Munich that the "Blaue Reiter" opened their first exhibition on 18 December 1911, and in 1912 it toured Germany. The "Blaue Reiter" were not an artists' association like the "Sturm." As Kandinsky put it in 1935: "In reality the "Blaue Reiter" were never an association or even a group, as is all too often, and erroneously, supposed. Marc and I simply took what we thought suitable, of our own free will...."

In 1909 yet another group, the "Künstlervereinigung München," was formed at Schwabing, the artists' quarter of Munich, the members being mostly French, Italians, Russians, Austrians, and Germans. The group included musicians, poets, dancers, and writers on art as well as artists. Early in 1911, however, internal dissensions made themselves felt, as a result of which Marc, Kandinsky, Kubin, and a number of others seceded. Marc wrote to his brother: "The die is cast. Kandinsky and I ... have left the group. Now there are only the two of us to carry on the fight. From now on the 'Blaue Reiter' will be launching a series of new exhibitions.... We shall try to become the center of the modern movement."

Kandinsky's idea of publishing a "yearbook" dates from June 1911. He communicated his idea to Marc. The original concept was a basically romantic synthesis of all the arts, embracing Symbol-

V Franz Marc: "Horses resting." Woodcut in three colors. 1912. 167 × 225 mm. Hand print. Lankheit 825.
The rhythm of this colored woodcut is an echo of "Jugendstil" ornamentation. Franz Marc did not take up wood-cuts till 1912, and this one is his first essay in this field. Previously he had confined himself to lithographs. The black-plate of this woodcut was published in "Der Sturm" in 1913.

V FRANZ MARC

ism, Russian mysticism, Art Nouveau aesthetics, Husserl's "Wesensschau," and the philosophy of Bergson. The 1912 yearbook was to be an illustration of this synthesis. It was to contain examples of Egyptian and East Asiatic art, and contributions from children and amateurs as well as articles on music and literature. The second "Blaue Reiter" exhibition in March 1912 was devoted entirely to the graphic arts: watercolors, drawings, and prints by Braque, Derain, de la Fresnaye, Picasso, Vlaminck, and "Die Brücke" painters, and the Russians Larionoff, Goncharova, and Malevitch. Other contributors included individualists such as Morgner and Georg Tappert, while the "Blaue Reiter" were represented by Klee, Kubin, Marc, Macke, Campendonk, and Kandinsky. The leading light was Kandinsky, who confessed in his *Selbstcharakteristik* (1918–1919) that "I regard the last years of the nineteenth century and the first of the twentieth as the dawn of one of the greatest intellectual epochs in the history of mankind, the epoch of a great spiritual upsurge." To the artists of his period, painting came first and foremost, and only Franz Marc contributed anything substantial in the way of prints. They were obviously influenced by Orphism and Futurism, two movements which Marc took to as avidly as he did to other phenomena of this particular period. The same versatility characterized all the other like-minded artists who were trying to form the kind of loose association that Herwarth Walden had built up with his periodical "Der Sturm" which had been appearing in a new form since 1910. He extended the term "Expressionism" to cover virtually all contemporary art, though it cannot be unreservedly applied to the Munich artists. In an introduction to the catalogue of the one hundredth "Sturm" exhibition in Berlin in 1921, Rudolf Blümner wrote that "Der Sturm" had never precisely defined the direction in which it was moving. "As a form of 'absolute,' i. e., pure art, it allows the artist a freedom which knows no other bounds than those of the artistic idea itself. These bounds are instinctively perceived but not defined, and as they can be communicated, whereas an artistic vision cannot, it follows that within them there can be no movement, school or academy. . . ." And in 1912, Herwarth Walden, for whom Kokoschka did his "Porträt der Woche" that is the very epitome of Expressionist portrait painting, had introduced the "Blaue Reiter" artists as well as Campendonk, Jawlensky, and Gabriele Münter as "Munich" artists in a loose sense, not to mention "French Expressionists" such as Braque, Derain, Othon Friesz, Herbin, Marie Laurencin, and Maurice de Vlaminck.

In April 1911, Marc had written to Macke that of the French artists, "The only ones I find interesting and serious are Friesz and Derain." But in Berlin "Der Sturm" had also exhibited Chagall, Gleizes, Léger, Picasso, and Delaunay, as well as the Futurists Boccioni, Carrá, and Severini. The

"Pathetiker," Ludwig Meidner and Jakob Steinhardt, were also exhibited under the auspices of "Der Sturm."

From the very first, the Munich artists tried to strike the same international note as "Der Sturm." Individual Munich artists therefore developed along totally different lines from those of the members of "Die Brücke," and so produced totally different results. Kandinsky's relationship to Expressionism was no more than a brief flirtation, a transition from an illustrative, romantic Art Nouveau style to an abstract form of art, dissociated from the world of sense perception, that was by and large contemporary with the "Blaue Reiter." Franz Marc, a pantheist and lyrical nature lover, regarded himself as the heir of a romantic heritage. As Herwarth Walden put it, "It was as if animals, woods, and stones, nay the whole earth, actually spoke to him. Though they know not what they do, they are the essential meaning of the world, and it was he who gave them the symbol, the parable."

The "Blaue Reiter" and "Sturm" groups professed totally different interpretations of the somewhat rigid term "Expressionism," although all artists who aimed at "going back to the beginning like a child" (Marc), the Germans as well as the French and Italians, started from the same premise. Kandinsky's notion of "dematerializing one's idea of the world" was also to a certain extent shared by the Cubists. But as time went on Expressionism enlarged its scope; on many artists it was to act as a stimulant for many years to come, and its ramifications manifested themselves in all sorts of different ways.

"Expressionism" can be taken to mean an inclination to exaggerate personal experiences and feelings into a world which is not limited to the depiction of perceptible phenomena but uses them to provoke individual and essentially subjective impressions. Acceptance of this definition implies a recognition that many trends in twentieth-century art can be loosely, but not dogmatically, classified as "Expressionism." But not unreservedly. One outstanding characteristic of Expressionist art is a predilection for deliberate exaggerations and distortions, a defiance of normal delineation and deployment that instead of aiming at harmonious proportions exults in exclamatory exuberance and deliberately sets out to shock, to enrapture, or to castigate. A letter from Wilhelm Morgner to Georg Tappert dated February 1912 is a typical illustration of an Expressionist artist's state of mind: "I live like fire, a fire that is aglow within me, more glowing than the superlative of the uttermost superlative could possibly express. My whole being is consumed with a flaring, hammering urgency as if my body had wings. I am devoured by a fiery frenzy that is ineffably infinite.

My ego is sloughing off its pall of inhibition, bursting its bonds. My very soul is seething, and I often feel I am about to explode like a charge of dynamite. And I am even more highly charged when I cease to perceive the outward manifestations of life and cease to confront them as illusions but give rein to the innermost workings of my will.... Yet when I return to an apparent awareness of my fellow-men the frenzy returns, and I have to restrain myself from slitting them open with a knife. It is the same with everyone I meet: I feel I must go for them. My whole being is a compound of molten frenzy and madness. The purest form of truth is life. Life is the only truth, everything else is an illusion . . . ."

If ravings of this sort can be taken as typical of Expressionism, it becomes virtually impossible to reconcile it with certain artists usually classified as "Expressionist." For one thing, even the Fauvists, albeit below the surface, professed a regard for clear distinctions and classifications (even in an anticlassical guise), which was why their aims were quite different from those of their German contemporaries and why they cannot be unreservedly classified as Expressionists. One can see too how in these years of revolution, of new departures and aspirations which affected all artists who had eyes to see and ears to hear, other influences were also clamoring for attention.

Offshoots

In the case of Oskar Kokoschka, it is the Austrian baroque element that gives his work its peculiar richness but at the same time debars it from fitting into any definite category. Similarly, the classical, lyrical symbolism of Wilhelm Lehmbruck, the realism of Käthe Kollwitz, and the classicism of Carl Hofer disqualify these artists from being labeled with any particular "ism." Even artists such as Ernst Barlach, Lyonel Feininger, Alfred Kubin, or Max Beckmann are too versatile and too individual to be classified exclusively as "Expressionists," though they all have certain features in common which mark them as belonging to a definite period. It begins to look then as if the term "Expressionist" is merely a convenient epithet for artists who had certain characteristic features in common but continued to go their own way within a definite period. The term can only be applied unreservedly to relatively few artists, or to a relatively brief period within the total span of certain artists' creative careers. Herbert Read regarded Realism, Expressionism, and Idealism as the three most important methods of expression. Hartlaub, however, maintained that a work of art can only be described as "Expressionist" if "the gap between the actual object and the artist's personal view of it" is exceptionally wide. He also distinguished between primary and secondary, between un-

62

conscious and deliberate, between pre-realistic and post-realistic (or post-idealistic) forms of Expressionism. But as in the case of all artistic periods, the vital impulse came not from any "trend" but from the influence of the individual artist on the work of others.

Be that as it may, it is extremely interesting to trace the various shades of deviation from strict Expressionism that began to manifest themselves after the First World War, during the transition to what has been called "new objectivity" or "magic realism." The works which Otto Dix or George Grosz, for instance, turned out during the 1920s are fundamentally different from those of the "Brücke" group. Yet it was precisely these two artists who elaborated definitely Expressionistic trends, and in their graphic work it is the critical, minatory element that looms largest. The same is true of Max Beckmann, who used many of his etchings, lithographs, and woodcuts for large-scale paintings. He once admitted that "to me, everything looks either black or white, like vice or virtue" (see page 129). Beckmann worshiped accuracy, simplicity, and economy. Eschewing "prettiness" and refinements of technique, his work has a certain roughness about it, because for him, and for a good many of his contemporaries too, art was first and foremost a human and not an aesthetic problem. George Grosz, for instance, declared that for him art was not a matter of aesthetics at all: "Drawing must be subordinated to a sense of social purpose. I mean, a preliminary sketch by a cabinetmaker is more practical, and in the last analysis more aesthetically beautiful, than an abstract, highly individual and almost invariably imprecise graphic representation of some obscure mystical experience...."

A change of direction

Grosz's recourse to phrases such as "highly individual and... imprecise graphic representation" and "some obscure mystical experience" are typical of the skeptical attitude towards traditional features of Expressionism that became the fashion after the First World War. It was a critical juncture for the Expressionist movement, brought about by the experiences on active service of Beckmann, Dix, Grosz, and Heckel, not to mention Oskar Kokoschka, who was severely wounded on the Russian front. Something had changed. The original enthusiasm for the "shock effect of the unusual" (Gahlen), for a more or less uncritical acceptance of anything which seemed to correspond to a "cosmic view of the world," had waned. The delight in originality and revolutionary ideas had been doused by the appalling experiences undergone by artists who had hoped that their work would be instrumental in bringing the machinery of war to a standstill, or even in putting it into reverse. As early as 1916 Kurt Hiller wrote in *Das Ziel* that a man who, metaphysically speaking, is a failure (i. e., "anyone who is really honest with himself") tends to take refuge in art. And again: "Art allows him to give vent to his spiritual torment. Art has something delightfully non-committal about it: one may play at metaphysics in art without being in any way committed to truth." A somewhat bitter view, perhaps, but one that was borne out by the work of most artists of a realistic turn of mind. There was a new trend towards less distortion, but the "new objectivity," for a time at any rate, was more of a slogan than an actual style. It absorbed post-Expressionism, Realism, and even the first essays in Surrealism. It was a phase that many important artists went through during the early 1920s.

Ivan Goll wrote in 1921: "Expressionism is on its last legs, but who was not touched by it at one time or another? We all were. Not a single Expressionist was a reactionary, not a single Expressionist was not anti-war, not a single Expressionist refused to believe in 'brotherhood' and 'the community.' In painting too... Expressionism was a good and important phase, the solidarity of all thinking people, a display of all that is genuine." Yet at almost exactly the same time Wilhelm Worringer, whose *Abstraktion und Einfühlung* (1907) exerted a profound influence on the early Expressionists by identifying a state of anxiety as the origin of all artistic creation, was maintaining that "if there had been any real originality behind all the paintings that exuded such a semblance of it, nobody would have lasted a second in an atmosphere so charged with explosive possibilities."

In short, the first rapture had evaporated, and it was in a mood of utter disenchantment that artists contemplated the grisly effects of war on the intellectual life of Europe. Few shared the hopes of

Kurt Pinthus (while still on active service in 1918) that it was the artist who "would lead mankind into the future, pointing the way ahead to a new life."

No sooner were the guns silent than new art societies were springing up almost overnight, notably the "Novembergruppe 1918" of Pechstein, Klein, Mueller, Campendonk, Purrmann, and others. But though they attracted considerable attention with their exhibitions in Berlin they could not avert the end of the great days of "the ecstatic break-out from the mental and physical prison of yesterday," a prison that was to be followed all too soon by "a new and even more hideous captivity." Powerless to divert the course of events, artists gave up the struggle. Many of them lost the creative powers that had once inspired even relatively minor talents to great achievements. It was not National Socialism that put an end to "degenerate art": it had long outlived its time anyway, even though its propagation, albeit in a diluted form, was only just beginning.

Yet certain forms of Expressionism continued to flourish, notably the graphic arts in general and woodcuts in particular. None of the artists who turned to woodcuts from about 1925 onwards could fail to be aware of what the "Brücke" group were still turning out, especially the more progressive elements such as Ernst Ludwig Kirchner. Kirchner was one of the few who had the strength and courage to continue on his way without constantly making fresh starts. Others, notably Lyonel Feininger, developed as graphic artists after the War by modifying what might be termed the "classical" Expressionistic style with certain facets that gave their work an unmistakable individuality. In about 1910 Feininger was still producing etchings that recalled his days as a caricaturist and the pioneer of artistic "comic strips," and it was not until after his protracted periods of study in Berlin and Paris that he embarked upon his characteristic wood engravings that displayed all the dynamic distortions and exaggerations of line and perspective that are so typical of the early stages of Expressionist art. Later, he developed a sort of crystalline precision rooted in a sensitivity that was essentially romantic in the manner of Caspar David Friedrich. What emerges most clearly from Feininger's work is his pronounced musicality and his keen sense of dimension, which enabled him to depict cosmic elements such as space and movement with purely one-dimensional media.

As for Beckmann, "he staggered through the postwar years as if they were the early days after the Flood," as Benno Reifenberg, one of his biographers, put it. "The distorted features of his figures are on a par with his devastated landscapes. He specialized in depicting the grimaces of the masses. Although the works of the early 1920s may well constitute a damning indictment of the deplorable state of society at that time, Beckmann's work is definitely not illustrative, nor did he have

VI EMIL NOLDE

Wilhelm Morgner: *Field and woman.*
Woodcut, 1912. 375 x 570 mm. Tappert 22.
This is a striking example of Morgner's
obsession with the abstract.

recourse to literary painting. What he did was to transform. He exposed ugliness in all its details, and while depicting horror he also depicted the anguish of those who had to contemplate it."

Beckmann's first graphic work that can really be classified as Expressionist is his well-known dry-point etching "Weinende Frau" (Weeping Woman) of 1914. There followed in 1915 the series of important graphic works that were based on his wartime experiences and were to exert a decisive influence on his future development. "Die Auferstehung" (The Resurrection) of 1918 is a typical example of the wealth of figures and background that was also characteristic of the "gothic," vertically compact content of many of his paintings. Both in concept and execution this etching goes far beyond the confines of Expressionism. All Beckmann's important works date from between 1912 and 1923, i. e., during the heyday of Expressionism. But his influence lasted a great deal longer.

Another artist who represented the abandonment of dramatic exclamation in favor of a more realistic style and a more definable content (as in Max Beckmann's postwar graphic work, and occasionally in the "new objectivity movement") was Otto Dix. Otto Conzelmann described how Dix's graphic works, ranging from dry-point etchings to aquatints, differed from the wartime drawings from which they originated. "Expressionist elements have made way for a scrupulous exactitude, and the original spontaneity has become a detached irony, and sometimes a macabre sort of humor. Instead of primitive simplification there is the utmost refinement; instead of visions there is cold calculation; instead of genuine feeling there is an exaggerated naturalism that delights in gruesome mutilations, horrific death throes, and the stink of decay; repulsive scenes that would be unbearable but for the masterly technique with which they are executed."

Individualists

The two strongest influences, Realism and Naturalism, served as links as well as points of departure, and even encroached on classical Expressionism. Their mutual relationship is still as close as ever, though the emphasis tends to shift from one to the other at different periods. Their influence ranges from pre- and post-Impressionism to pop art, which itself makes use of Expressionist elements, to revolutionary artists from Central and South America, and to artists like Gyula Derkovits in Hungary who adapted Expressionism to their own purposes. The Realists soon learned how to make the best use of the salient features of Expressionism, while the post-Expressionists established close contact with the Realists. Nowhere is this more apparent than in the domain of graphic art in general, and in the work of Käthe Kollwitz in particular. She started out from Naturalism, which was the basis of all her work, being strongly of the opinion that Naturalism was her only hope of recognition. Her use of Expressionist elements is most pronounced in her woodcuts, though she herself stoutly denied that she was an Expressionist. "The human form must be stripped of all extraneous accretions": in other words, it must be simple and concentrated. The fact remains, however, that as far as a good deal of her work is concerned, Käthe Kollwitz must be classified as an Expressionist simply because the humanity and sympathy which are such prominent features of her work are the very same qualities that are most characteristic of so many Expressionist artists. The gulf between her work and theirs is not very wide.

Three other highly individual artists were Ernst Barlach, Christian Rohlfs, and Alfred Kubin. Barlach's graphic works are closely akin to sculpture, and his favorite material is wood. In all his work there is a strong symbolic, mystical element, and his extensive travels in Russia long before World War I exerted an abiding influence.

Christian Rohlfs, who was a good deal older than the other artists with whom he shared exhibitions, became acquainted with Edvard Munch in 1897 and with Emil Nolde in 1905, yet it was not until 1908, at the age of fifty-nine, that he produced his first woodcuts. Alfred Kubin was first and foremost a draftsman, even in his lithographs, which he regarded as means of reproduction rather than a form of art in their own right. In this he differed from Kokoschka, who was also an out-and-out individualist but attracted attention at an early stage in his career with his series of visionary graphic works. Despite his woodcuts and etchings, his favorite medium is still crayon lithography, and his supreme mastery of this technique is attested by his "Der gefesselte Columbus" (Columbus in chains) which dates from as far back as 1913.

70

Alfred Kubin: *In memoriam Dostoievsky (near the frontier)*. Lithograph, 1919. 203 x 160 mm. Raabe 1957, No 114. Kubin's style and imagination were outstanding features of this particular chapter in the history of art.

Ernst Barlach: *Dead children*. Woodcut, 1919. 240 x 360 mm. Schult 1957. This is one of ten woodcuts completed in 1919 illustrating the horrors of war: starvation, destitution, death, homelessness. Käthe Kollwitz wrote in her diary: "I have seen something which bowled me over: Barlach's woodcuts. Barlach knows where he is going; I don't."

Syntheses

Generations of artists came at one time or another under the spell of Expressionism, though as time went on its influence waned. Yet Expressionism is still very much alive and has given rise, especially among French artists, to "synthetic" works which combine Expressionist elements with features of later trends, particularly in the case of Dufresne, the early Braque, Picasso, Lyonel Feininger, Oskar Kokoschka, Max Beckmann, Otto Dix, and in the early works of Kirchner. One or two late Expressionist works reveal retrograde tendencies which in the case of Kokoschka place him alongside the Impressionists or painters such as Lovis Corinth. With Heckel these retrograde tendencies took the form of a sort of romantic realism, while Otto Dix, too, eventually turned the clock back. The evaporation of the first ecstatic rapture which characterized the early Expressionists led to a search for a new firm basis that would enable Expressionism to survive an age in which the revolutionary mood had been dispersed by a wind of change that was middle-class rather than revolutionary. Individual styles either degenerated into mannerisms or accepted noncommittal compromises that were prepared to abandon the impetus and originality of the early years.

18 LUDWIG MEIDNER, *Prophet*. Lithograph. 1918. 520 x 395 mm.

The powerful movement, the emotionalism, the lamentation and imploring of the Expressionists all find their classic expression here. Meidner is better known as an etcher, whose lithographs were only a side-line. Like Kokoschka he made portraits of many of his fellow-rebels and other contemporaries.

19 KARL SCHMIDT-ROTTLUFF, *Girl from Kovno*. Woodcut. 1918. 503 x 390 mm. Schapiro 209.

The influence of Negro sculpture, so evident here, is particularly preponderant in Schmidt-Rottluff's prints.

20 CESAR KLEIN, *Woman*. Woodcut. 278 x 337 mm.

21 OTTO LANGE, *Woman with rooster*. Color-woodcut, 1919. 609 x 445 mm.

The woodcuts of Klein and Lange bring out various possibilities which were developed further by less inventive and talented artists under the spell of their greatness. The basis on which the Expressionists worked was at one time very wide.

22 CONRAD FELIXMÜLLER, *Café-billard*. Etching. 1914. 248 x 117 mm. Reproduced original size.

Reminiscent of Van Gogh's café pictures from Arles, but the sketched-in suggestion of the cold emptiness of the room is, if possible, even more effective here. Felixmüller produced numerous prints in series or as illustrations.

23 JAKOB STEINHARDT, *Fight in Russian town*. Dry-point etching. 1913. 133 x 193 mm. Reproduced original size.

Steinhardt is another of the forgotten men of his day. Yet precisely this etching affords striking proof of his premonition of the approaching storm, of the horrors impending, which were recorded by other artists, but generally only after the event. In the same year he produced a woodcut, related to this etching, under the title "Pogrom."

24 CARL CRODEL, *Curve*. Woodcut. 1920. 200 x 185 mm.

25 RICHARD SEEWALD, *Sodom and Gomorrha*. Colored woodcut. 1914. 212 x 304 mm.

26 CARL HOFER, *Shipwreck II*. Lithograph. 456 x 379 mm.

One of the more Expressionistic works of this artist, who is otherwise, like Lehmbruck, more interested in the calm, classical style.

27 OSKAR KOKOSCHKA, *Resurrection*. Lithograph. 1916. 260 x 305 mm. Arntz 58.

The contrast between this work and that of Beckmann shows how differently two contemporaries may experience one and the same allegory-type subject. One might describe the effects produced as baroque and gothic respectively.

28 MAX BECKMANN, *Resurrection*. Dry-point etching. 1918. 238 x 332 mm. Glaser 113, Gallwitz 103b. Pre-edition print (G. Franke Collection, Munich).

From 1916 to 1918 Beckmann was working on a large painting with the title "Resurrection," but it remained unfinished. He also made a drawing on this subject. He combined personal experiences with wartime occurrences to make an impressive spectacle, and thus recorded a commentary on the times.

29 JOHN MARIN, *Woolworth Building No 3*. Etching. 1913. 327 x 263 mm. Zigrosser 115.

The subtitle "The Dance" is justified by the way the skyscrapers and trees appear to be gyrating round one another in an explosive approach. "Because these buildings move me," Marin said in connection with his New York print-series, "I attempt to express the movement around me . . . so that I may recall the spell I have been under, and behold the expression of the different emotions that have been called into being."

30 LYONEL FEININGER, *Buildings*. Woodcut. 1919. 469 x 368 mm.
The way in which the pattern of the architecture is spread in a rhythmical movement over the whole picture-surface is typical.

31 OTTO DIX, *Soldiers from the front in Brussels*. Etching and wash. 1924. 286 x 198 mm. Löffler 66.
From the fourth war-folio (see text, pp 16 and 65 f).

32 GEORGE GROSZ, *The convict*. Lithograph. 463 x 345 mm.
The post-war urban environment which this artist rendered in his incomparable sarcastic manner. His scenery is complex, and falls between Verism and Expressionism, with a futuristic trend.

33 OTTO MUELLER, *Two girls bathing*. Lithograph. 1922. 392 x 288 mm. Karsch 143.
The theme of human figures in a landscape was constantly repeated and varied by this artist. His moderately Expressionist, restrained style underwent very little development, but he took all the more joy in technical experiments.

34 KÄTHE KOLLWITZ, *Death and woman fighting for child*. Etching. 1911. 226 x 285 mm. Klipstein 118/IX.
Something of the wearisome process of bringing an etching to perfection is exemplified in this work, of which nine states exist. Again and again the artist added and corrected, etched and worked with the dry point, polished and ground out, then covered the polished-out surfaces with fresh strokes. The resultant print is extremely rich in nuances. A first edition appeared in 1920, and further editions were printed from 1931 onwards. Käthe Kollwitz worked out this subject several times, and a number of versions such as the "Farewell" of 1910 (Klipstein 113) are in existence. This artist produced numerous print cycles, and a total of 270 individual prints, among which lithographs predominate.

35 JOSEF HEGENBARTH, *Procession*. Dry-point etching. 1920. 323 x 222 mm.
Here the artist has produced a highly personal achievement, utilizing various means of heightening the expressiveness, which is not typical of his later work. Its Expressionist impulse derives without question from the times in which it was executed.

18 LUDWIG MEIDNER

19 KARL SCHMIDT-
ROTTLUFF

20 CESAR KLEIN

21 OTTO LANGE

22 CONRAD FELIXMÜLLER   23 JAKOB STEINHARDT

24 CHARLES
CRODEL

25 RICHARD
SEEWALD

Schiffbruch II.   Hofer

26 CARL HOFER

27 OSKAR KOKOSCHKA

28 MAX BECKMANN

—Woolworth— —Marin '13

31 OTTO DIX

32 GEORGE GROSZ

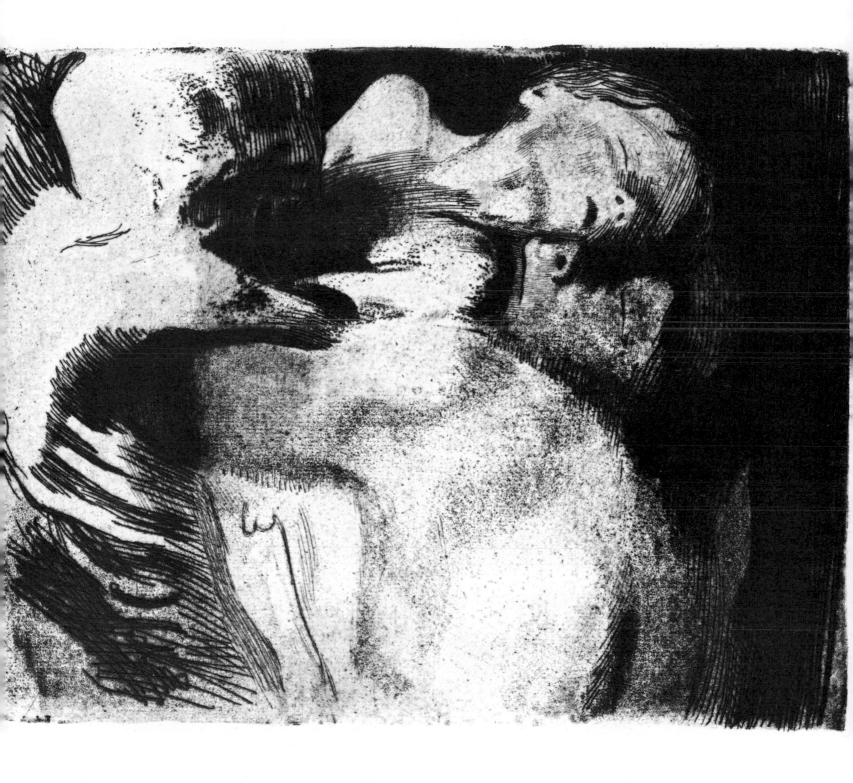

33 OTTO MUELLER   34 KÄTHE KOLLWITZ

35 JOSEF HEGENBARTH

Expressionism and Revolution

During the years immediately succeeding the First World War, Expressionism, or derivatives of Expressionism, obtained a foothold in almost all European countries. In many cases there was a nationalistic tinge – Belgian, Swiss, Austrian, Czech, for instance – while in Italy the Futurists played up the revolutionary element. Hardly any country in Europe was unaffected by the wind of change in the artistic world, and in many cases the new trends in art were faithful reflections of far-reaching political upheavals, notably in Russia, though the Russian contribution to the history of Expressionism was not of any great importance and in the domain of graphic art was little more than desultory. The first "Fauves" exhibition in Moscow in 1907 inspired a sort of Russian Fauvism headed by Michael Larionoff, who later, with the help of his wife, Natalia Contcharova, founded "Rayonism," a technique by which landscape and figures were reduced to radial patterns. It was he who in 1912 issued the celebrated "Rayonist Manifesto." A Russian group of Futurists had come into being in 1910, but for nearly all Russian artists Expressionism and its ancillary movements were no more than a transition stage. Some of them evolved a style of their own influenced by East European Judaism and a mystic view of the world, notably Marc Chagall, who contributed to the "Sturm" exhibition in 1914 and in his early years drifted very close to Expressionist influences, and Jules Pascin, a Bulgarian by birth and one of the "peintres maudits" who landed in Paris by way of Vienna and Munich. Like most French artists, Chaim Soutine, who developed the Fauve style along lines of his own and settled in Paris in 1913, was primarily a painter and not a graphic artist.

The Moscow group's most important link was with Kandinsky in Munich. Kandinsky too developed his own brand of Expressionism with a strong Russian flavor, and in 1912 he invited Larionoff, Natalia Contcharova, Malevich, and the Burliuk brothers to contribute to the second "Blaue Reiter" exhibition in Munich in March 1912. Alexei von Jawlensky, whose graphic œuvre makes up in quality for what it lacks in quantity, fell at an early stage under the influence of Van Gogh and Matisse, and was much closer to the French than to the German school. In his graphic works he favored simplicity of form elaborated with symbolic arabesques. According to Haftmann his artistic mentors were "Kandinsky, the Russians, Matisse, and Matisse à la Gauguin."

Consequences

The great changes wrought by Expressionism in the domains of literature, music, and the theater as well as in art attracted a number of minor talents who every now and then produced something exceptional but on the whole lacked the sustained power to maintain the high standards set by the pioneers or to develop personalities of their own. Style degenerated into mannerisms, dictated by whatever happened to be fashionable at the time.

The crisis in the Expressionist movement came to a head shortly after the end of the First World War, when the world was beginning to sober up after the turmoil and upheavals of the war years. In the artistic world the general trend was reflected in the "New Objectivity" and "Bauhaus" movements, both of which aimed at restraining the Expressionists' uncontrolled emotional outbursts and (to start with at any rate) at combining Expressionist with constructive trends. Later, the Bauhaus was also at pains to lay the foundations of a new functional pattern. On the other hand, the Expressionists can be regarded as the originators of the antisocial and anticultural (e. g., Futurist) trends of the time, as eventually expressed by the Dadaists and certain aspects of Surrealism. One thing all these postwar movements had in common was a mood of revolt against a precarious social structure that showed every sign of imminent disintegration. So Expressionism and its aftermath, though apparently contradictory, can be regarded as the beginning of the process as a result of which "dogmatic and programmatic styles, based on psychological considerations and defiantly sloughing off tradition, made a fresh start and at the same time stepped up the shock-effect of the unusual. By virtue of its infinite subjective variety, this movement manifested itself in an almost equally infinite variety of derivations, and is the essential substance of what we nowadays call 'modern' art" (Arnold Gehlen).

In Central Europe, which exerted considerable influence on American art, post-Expressionist trends of one kind or another kept recurring. There were, for instance, the "Cobra Group" in Holland, Asger Jorn in Scandinavia, the "Art-Brut" group founded by Jean Dubuffet, the Spaniard Antonio Saura, and the informal and abstract Expressionism of the Americans which revived trends that Kandinsky had anticipated in his "transition to abstract painting." "Happenings" are also a form of Expressionism, and contemporary woodcuts are much closer to Expressionism than to other forms of art.

Many European artists developed variations of Expressionism without being unfaithful to its original tenets. But the revolutionary element that is part and parcel of Expressionism flared most brightly in a country far from Europe where political revolutions were almost a daily occurrence at that time – in Mexico.

Mikhail Fiodorovitch Larionoff: Lithograph, 1912. 127 x 165 mm. The simplicity and effectiveness of the Russians' style differ notably from the work of their Western contemporaries.

Revolutionary graphic art in Mexico

The German Expressionists and the Fauves had modeled their one-side prints, especially their early woodcuts, on the simple illustrated stories (picture sheets) that were still being produced during the nineteenth century at Epinal and Neuruppin for the man in the street who could not read but responded to pictures. Similarly, a Mexican schoolmaster who had taught himself to paint realized very early in his career how easy it would be to entertain and at the same time educate the illiterate masses by simple one-side prints. José Guadalupe Posada made his way to Mexico City in 1887 and was taken on by a publisher to turn out a regular series of pencil drawings or zinc-etchings of current events. His primitive technique was all that could be expected of an individual brought up on folklore, but his directness, his imagination, and above all his choice of subject entitle some of his small-scale works to challenge comparison with Goya's. He was looked up to as a master by Rivera and Orozco, who carried on where he left off; and he can certainly be regarded as one of the precursors of twentieth-century Expressionism, even though, far from exerting any influence on European painters, he merely adopted the kind of ornamental "art nouveau" that had secured more than just a foothold in Mexico. Posada's style "gradually became freer and more human without jettisoning an iota of the exaggerated emotionalism of his Spanish-American environment; indeed, he positively personified all the stoic, romantic, tragic, dramatic, and even melodramatic elements in the Mexican make-up" (Armin Haab).

Posada is generally regarded as the pioneer of Mexican graphic art, and he was undoubtedly one of the founders of modern Mexican art. The fifteen thousand separate works that he completed by 1913 are illustrations of contemporary events in what is known as "Calaveras" style. About ten years after Posada's death, Rivera, who had returned to Mexico in 1922 after a long stay in France, joined Orozco and Siqueiros in glorifying the Mexican Revolution with a series of large scale murals. In 1937 they set up what they called a "Taller de gráfica popular" (literally, "a workshop of popular graphic art"), which comprised most of Mexico's leading exponents of the graphic arts. Like "Die Brücke" in its early years, the "Taller" stipulated that its members should work together and draw no distinctions between social and artistic ends. Traditional Spanish influences were discarded in favor of the native Indian idiom. The "Taller's" most striking product was an anti-Franco, anti-Hitler, and anti-Yankee-imperialism series of woodcuts on the popular lines laid down by Posada.

José Guadalupe Posada, Corrido: *The end of the world*. 210 x 117 mm. Only about 500 of close to 15,000 zinc etchings and lead and iron-cuts by Posada have survived. His use of motifs from popular art is a clear anticipation of Expressionist trends.

In the domain of graphic art the Mexican Expressionists were by no means prolific, and Siqueiros's flirtation with lithography was of short duration, yet their realism is comparable with that of, say, Käthe Kollwitz. But during the late 1930s Orozco and Tamayo moved away from the other Expressionists and by adapting Picasso to their own environment produced a form of Expressionism that was peculiar to Mexico. From Mexico this hybrid Expressionist-Realist style spread to other Latin-American countries, and a new edition, so to speak, of what Mexican artists turned out between the two world wars can be found today in Cuba. Earlier, a form of Expressionism had been developed by the Cuban Wilfredo Lam (b. 1902) and the Chilean Roberto Sebastián Echaurren Matta (b. 1912).

The aftermath in France

By contributing to the "Salon d'automne 1905" exhibition, along with Matisse, Derain, and Manguin, Georges Rouault declared his allegiance to "Les Fauves." In about 1916 he started on his series of aquatint etchings entitled "Miserere et guerre" which was completed in 1927 but was not published (under the title "Miserere") until 1948. Its origin was a complicated process, half-mechanical and half-manual. What Rouault did was to transfer his *gouache* sketches onto copper plates by a photographic process, and the resulting heliogravures were then worked on by a positive arsenal of instruments, which was why the process was such a lengthy one. In Rouault's own words, "I was never satisfied, but restarted from scratch over and over again, often producing 12 or 15 states of the same sketch." The Expressionist element, though palpable, is different from German Expressionism: it is softer, more akin to the Expressionism of the painters, with a wealth of detail and nuances, though the heads and figures are delineated with almost sculptural clarity. The series as a whole must be regarded as one of the most striking manifestations of European Expressionism. The fifty-eight etchings are a vivid depiction of Rouault's harrowing experiences in the First World War, and the symbolism is enhanced by a sort of mystical chiaroscuro, as in an icon.

At first sight, an artist like Marcel Gromaire would seem to bear some affinity to Rouault, even though his preference for making his figures stand out against a blurred background was totally different from Rouault's work. The outstanding characteristic of his work is an expressive realism that places him alongside Fernand Léger and has no parallel in French art with the possible exception of the opportunist extravagances of, say, Bernard Buffet.

Maurice de Vlaminck: *Three women in a brothel.*
Woodcut, about 1905. 223 x 178 mm.

The one artist who has really made a contribution of inestimable value to twentieth-century art is Pablo Picasso. Cutting clean across styles and movements he imbued Expressionist ideals with fresh vitality and validity. Few of his early etchings bear any relation to what his contemporaries were turning out. His personal brand of Expressionism did not unfold until he had (at any rate temporarily) turned his back on his "classical" period and evolved a style embracing critical sympathy and a sort of agitation that is all his own. In his "Bull and Minotaur" series of about 1934 he hit upon a style that he repeated in the two "Franco's Dream and Lies," aquatint etchings that constituted his devastating verdict on the Spanish Civil War. From then on Picasso developed his own version of Expressionism in a series of studies of female heads that are "out of drawing" and grossly distorted. The "Franco's Dreams and Lies" etchings on the other hand are a classic example of graphic art in the service of propaganda. They were originally intended to be reproduced in postcard format, but later on Picasso changed his mind. The various scenes are full of symbolism and obscure references, and the same element of caricature recurs in the work of the German late-Expressionists.

Post-Expressionism

It very soon became abundantly clear that "Classical Expressionism" existed only in theory, and that in actual fact subjective artists (like all Expressionists) were being influenced by all sorts of different trends and styles. With Carl Hofer it was idealism, with Max Beckmann a "transcendental realism," and with Kokoschka a dramatic form of Impressionism. Pure Expressionism was still further watered down by developments that set in in the 1920s but were temporarily obliterated by the Nazi and Fascist idea of what constituted the "good taste of the man in the street," who was alleged to be resolutely opposed not only to Expressionism but all forms of what was termed "degenerate art." Hardly a single artist ever recaptured the rapture of the early days between "Die Brücke" and its counterpart Kandinsky. By and large, however, the early Expressionists and all the other artists who were seeking new methods of expressing themselves more or less freely managed to find some way of doing so.

The artists who contributed most to propagating Expressionism were the ones who seized on, developed, and modified what the great names had initiated. In the domain of graphic art, names such as Otto Lange (1879–1944), Max Kaus (b. 1891), Heinrich Nauen (1880–1940), Otto Pankok (b. 1893), and Max Unold (b. 1885) immediately come to mind. They were followed by illustrators of the caliber of Ewald Mataré (b. 1887), Gerhard Marcks (b. 1889), Hans Fronius (b. 1902), the early Karl Rössing (b. 1897), and K.-H. Hansen-Bahia (b. 1915). Among artists who kept at illustrative lithographs and woodcuts even after 1945 were Otto Dix, Josef Hegenbarth, Oskar Kokoschka, Alfred Kubin, Frans Masereel, and Richard Seewald.

After 1945, post-Expressionism branched out in fresh directions in the United States as well as in Europe, but without influencing the graphic arts as strongly as in the days of classical Expressionism. Between 1948 and 1950 a group of European artists formed an association with the aim of arriving at what they called "Expressionism of the fantastic" by means of action painting. They called themselves the "Cobra Group" after the native cities of their founders, Asger Jorn (Copenhagen), Corneille (Brussels), and Karel Appel (Amsterdam). Their symbols and figures were expressed in an elaborate and highly ornamental style that was taken up in other parts of Europe and can in many respects be compared with Jean Dubuffet's "art brut" in which drawings by children and lunatics figured prominently. While closely examining the works of Vincent van Gogh, James Ensor, and Edvard Munch, Eugene Bleuler had already established schizophrenic affinities, "the autistic world being the real world, and the other world only an illusion." In Kubin as well as in Ensor there are certain "manic" elements that fragmentate the composition as a whole. The same elements recur in the work of the "Cobra Group" and of later artists who deliberately depicted figments of the imagination.

The "Abstract Expressionism" that evolved in the United States had no influence, or at any rate no decisive influence, on prints. Eventually it led to what is understood in America by "action painting," which is akin to Kandinsky's early abstract works, his "improvisations," and adopted surrealistic and automatistic elements (Jackson Pollock). Its European counterpart was the "Quadriga" formed in 1952 by the painters K. O. Goetz (b. 1914), O. Greis (b. 1913), and B. Schultze (b. 1915), who were later joined by E. Schumacher (b. 1912). Their modification of "Abstract Expressionism" (in its graphic form) bears some relation to the work of artists such as K. R. H. Sonderborg (b. 1923), the Spaniard Antonio Saura (b. 1930), or the Italian Emilio Vedova (b. 1919).

The neo-Expressionist movement was kept alive by some young German artists from the school of Hap Grieshaber, a wood engraver who developed early Expressionist motifs along lines of his own. Similarly, the "supertemporal" form of Expressionism also found a style of its own in the work of Hans Baschang (b. 1937) and in Horst Antes's "Figur-Augenmensch," metamorphoses and paraphrases with allusions to Beckmann, Kirchner, Léger, and Picasso. Post-Expressionist trends were also kept alive in Austria by Alfred Hrdlicka (b. 1928), and Adolf Frohner (b. 1934). The woodcuts of another Austrian, Werner Berg, make no secret of his allegiance to the early Expressionists, and the admirable woodcuts of the American Leonard Baskin are clearly inspired by Ernst Barlach.

It is primarily in the domain of woodcuts that Expressionism is still very much alive all over the world. In 1969 the Italian town of Carpi, the birthplace of the celebrated wood engraver Ugo da Carpi (ca. 1480–1532), mounted its first international Triennial of contemporary woodcuts, some forty different countries contributing. The exhibition showed how widely the direct descendants of Expressionism are scattered all over the world. Expressionist wood engravers are hard at work from South Africa to Sweden and from Turkey to Canada and Uruguay and Australia. But how many of them will succeed in recapturing the verve of the pioneers in this field?

Max Beckmann: *A morgue*. Woodcut, 1923. 375 x 470 mm. Glaser 227, Gollwitz 221.

VII *Erich Heckel: "White horses." Woodcut in four colors. 1912. 238 x 251 mm. Dube 242.*
This woodcut exists in four states taken from two blocks in two different versions. "I imagine early Greek murals must have been something like this," Heckel wrote. "The atmosphere is of a sort of Dionysian burgeoning rather than Apollonian serenity. . . . It radiates a mood of carefree gaiety."

VIII *Wassily Kandinsky: "Bowman." Colored woodcut for "Klänge." 1908/09. 165 x 154 mm. Roethel 79. Original dimensions.*
"Klänge," a volume of thirty-eight prose poems, with twelve colored and forty-three black-and-white woodcuts in different styles and from different periods of Kandinsky's career, was published by Piper of Munich in 1913. This particular woodcut recalls the fairy-tale world of Kandinsky's earlier years. Some of its dramatic and dynamic elements verge on abstraction and are definitely Expressionistic.

Publishers and Collections

Much of the credit for the propagation of Expressionist prints must go to the publishers who in many cases commissioned whole series of prints or illustrations. One of the busiest publishers in this field was the Frenchman Ambroise Vollard, notable for the illustrative works he commissioned and for his sumptuous "Livres des peintres." The German publishers pursued a different course and were at pains to ensure that the illustrations matched the text as closely as possible, which is why they particularly favored woodcuts, which could be printed alongside the text. As early as 1907 Erich Heckel produced a series of ten woodcuts as illustrations for Oscar Wilde's "Ballad of Reading Gaol." Kirchner's finest series of woodcuts was a set of forty-seven illustrations (1924)

VII   ERICH HECKEL

VIII WASSILY KANDINSKY

Frans Masereel: Lithograph to "Fairfax" by Carl Sternheim. 1922. 290 x 230 mm.

for Georg Heym's "Umbra vitae." Among other artists who turned out illustrations of high quality were Ernst Barlach, who between 1911 and 1927 produced ten different series; Max Beckmann, with eleven series between 1909 and 1946; Oskar Kokoschka, with eight series between 1908 and 1918 and a number of others more recently; Otto Dix, with seven series between 1921 and 1924; and Georg Grosz, with seven series between 1921 and 1925. In 1918 Frans Masereel produced a series of twenty-five woodcuts entitled "The Passion of a Human Being," and a further series of 167 woodcuts entitled "My Book of Hours" appeared in the following year.

Among the owners of galleries who came out in favor of Expressionism from the very first were Alfred Flechtheim, Herwarth Walden, Karl Nierendorf, Paul Cassirer, and J. B. Neumann who published a number of works by Heckel and Kirchner. It was Nierendorf who in 1925 published the complete war etchings of Otto Dix in five issues (and with very little success).

Nearly all the original publishers of German Expressionist prints were forced to quit Central Europe when Expressionism was classified as "decadent art." Many Expressionist works were destroyed, and nearly all Expressionist artists were banned from painting.

After 1945, the market value of Expressionist prints rose steadily, and they began to fetch the kind of prices more often associated with paintings and drawings. This in turn led to a far-reaching reappraisal of prints as a form of art in their own right.

After the Second World War, nearly all the German collections had to start again from scratch, unlike the great national and private collections in Switzerland and the U.S.A. which turned the Nazi ban to their own advantage by acquiring many of the most important prints before the War. Today, the leading German collections of Expressionist prints are to be found in the two cities which from the turn of the century to the mid-1920s were the centers of German art: Munich (Staatliche Graphische Sammlungen and Städtische Galerie) and Dresden. There are also substantial collections in Berlin, Stuttgart, Hamburg, and Essen. Here, as in the great American museums, anyone who is interested in Expressionist prints can study original works to his heart's content.

110

Werner Berg: *Courtship*. Woodcut, about 1960. 415 x 545 mm. The severity and abrupt linear contrasts of line and surface of this late-Expressionist woodcut are relieved by the grain of the wood.

36 GEORGES ROUAULT, *Hiver lèpre de la terre*. Etching and wash. 1922. 515 x 367 mm. No 24 in the "Miserere" cycle.

37 JOSE CLEMENTE OROZCO, *Payaso*. Etching and wash. 1944. 270 x 170 mm. Marrozzini 43.
The influence of Picasso's graphic work of the Thirties is unmistakable.

38 PABLO PICASSO, *Sueño y Mentira de Franco*. Etching and wash. 1937. 310 x 420 mm. Bloch 297.

39 PABLO PICASSO, *Sueño y Mentira de Franco*. Etching and wash. 1937. 310 x 420 mm. Bloch 298. "Franco's Dream and Lie" provides the key to "Guernica." The bull, in numerous metamorphoses, is Franco's adversary, by whom he is destroyed. The references are explained in detail in Vol. 880 in the Insel Bücherei (Frankfurt-am-Main, 1968) with a text by Werner Spies to the sheets reproduced here.

40 RUFINO TAMAYO, *Figure*. Etching. About 1950. 201 x 150 mm. Reproduced original size.
A personal achievement in the combination of Expressionist-Cubist with archaic formal elements.

41 LEONARD BASKIN, *Haman*. Woodcut. 1956. 1120 x 580 mm.
Baskin sees the artist as observer, commentator, and prophet. His ancestry goes back to Callot, Blake, Bresdin, and Redon. In America he is considered the greatest natural genius in black and white art. He produced not only woodcuts, but also etchings, lithographs, drawings, and illustrations. Like Barlach, whom he admires, he also works as a sculptor.

42 MARCEL GROMAIRE, *In the Métro*. Etching. 1927. 177 x 129 mm.

43 HORST ANTES, *Couple*. Etching on zinc. 1964. 217 x 196 mm. Gercken 19.

44 ALFRED HRDLICKA, *The Newest Testament*, detail. Etching, roulette, and mezzotint in two colors. 1967. 745 x 542 mm. Sotriffer 146.

45 HAP GRIESHABER, *Couple*. Color-woodcut. 1963. 460 x 280 mm. Fürst 283 (see text, p 124).

46 DAVID ALFARO SEQUEIROS, *Zapata*. Lithograph. 1930. 536 x 401 mm.

47 ARNULF RAINER, *Mars*. Lithograph from the folio "Wahnhall." 1968. 320 x 493 mm. Breicha 46.

48 JOHANN HAUSER, Etching. 1968. 179 x 79 mm. Hauser is a patient at the Gugging Sanatorium of Lower Austria, near Klosterneuburg, where Leo Navratil has long taken an interest in the artistic productions of the patients in his charge, or has attempted to incite them to creative production. Hauser's work stimulated an artist like Arnulf Rainer, who deliberately maintains a close connection with "the art of the mentally deranged."

49 ASGER JORN, *Forgetting*. Lithograph in three colors. 1960-61. 500 x 350 mm.

50 JEAN DUBUFFET, *Figure in red costume*. Color-lithograph. 1961. 525 x 380 mm.
An example of the acceptance of primitive-expressionist structures from children's drawings and those of the mentally deranged by a contemporary artist for the purpose of clarifying the connection between creative activity and uncontrolled aesthetic phenomena. In this connection see also p 12.

GEORGES
ROUAULT

37 J. C. OROZCO

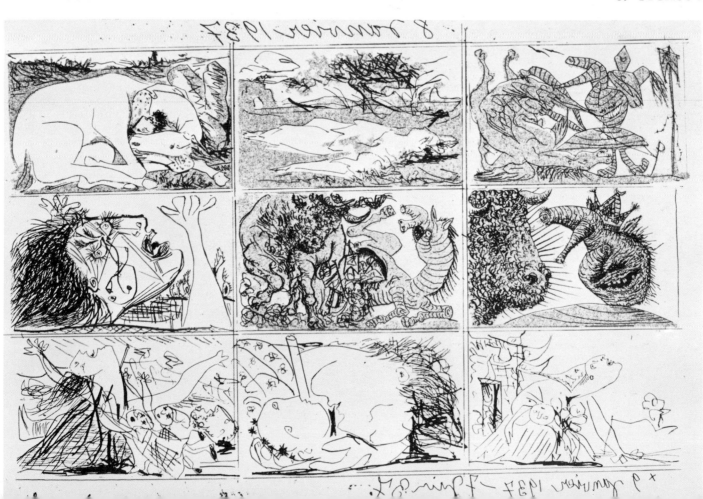

19/40

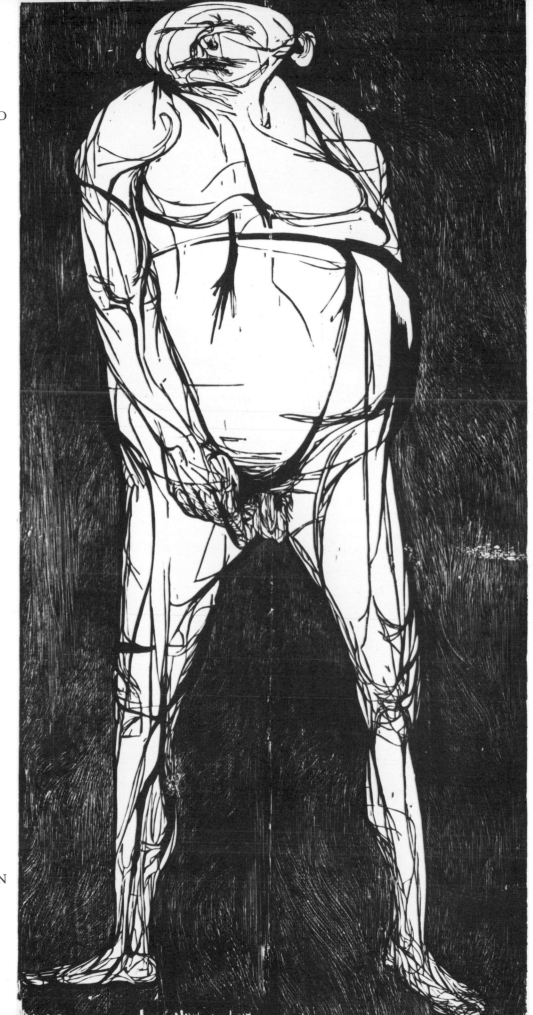

40 RUFINO TAMAYO

41 LEONARD BASKIN

42 GROMAIRE

43 ANTES

44 HRDLICKA

45 GRIESHABER

46
SIQUEIROS

48 HAUSER

47 RAINER

49 JORN   50 DUBUFFET

The Artists on themselves

ERNST LUDWIG KIRCHNER

It was probably Kirchner who made the most lasting impression on his close contemporaries, both as practical artist and as theorist. The following extracts are taken from his comments on his own work published under the pseudonym L. de Marsalle in the periodical "Genius" during the year 1921.

Lithography

"He goes on working on his stones until the original drawing has become entirely 'graphic,' that is to say until the drawn lines disappear and are freshly formed by etched marks. Deep blacks alternate with a silky grey produced by the grain of the stone. The soft tone-value of the grey areas formed by the grain has a colourful effect, giving warmth to the prints. In this way Kirchner has created his own technique in lithography, so much richer in effects than the woodcut. In addition to this he has devised for himself a color-process that permits him to print chromo-lithographs with any desired number of colour-plates, all from a single stone, whereby, using a process analogous to painting, he produces colour-prints of great charm. Each colour is independently worked out. The power of the designs of the single plates are combined in the final print, in which they appear one above the other. Kirchner's lithographs are only printed in very small editions; there exist only five, seven or at most ten edition-prints, and a number of impressions of different states. He has never worked on transfer-paper, from which unfortunately the majority of lithographs are made today, which makes them no more than reproduced drawings.... All his lithographs show the edge of the stone. For black-and-white work he favours lemon-yellow paper."

Woodcuts

"Kirchner produced his first prints about 1900 in the form of woodcuts. The woodcut is the most graphic of the graphic techniques. Great technical skill and interest are required for its practice. Kirchner's technical facility makes the production of woodcuts easy for him. Thus the simplification demanded by it led him spontaneously to a clear style in representation. In his woodcuts, which constantly accompany his creative work, the idiom of his pictures is preformed.... The vitality of his perceptiveness preserved him from the danger of that schematic quality that spoils most of the woodcuts of our times. In his early days he tried to use woodcuts in book-illustration. He was the first to have his plates printed together with the text (in 'Der Sturm,' 9/10 years) whereby he involuntarily initiated the contemporary flood of woodcut book-illustration. He himself had never previously succeeded in finding a publisher for his illustrations. He also experimented in cutting the letterpress together with the picture, in order to shape the page as a whole.... Along with simple black-and-white prints he created a series of colour-woodcuts. As a result of many experiments he succeeded in devising a new method of working with from two to ten plates without an outline-plate.... The colour-plates always cover the entire surface. Kirchner would never cut a plate for the sake of a different-coloured dot. Thus "Mann und Mädchen" [Man and Girl], for instance, is printed in three colours – blue-green, yellow, and orange – one on top of the other. Such colour-prints are genuinely composed in colour, and should be clearly distinguished from mere coloured black-and-white prints. There are prints of various states of works in a number of colours in which the grading of the different colours differs. Sometimes plates are omitted, sometimes such a test embodies more plates than does the edition. This shows how this artist experiments with the colour. A colour-print grows up like a painting. In printing Kirchner likes to utilize the elasticity of the wood. In this way the passages with blending colours arise.

"Although precisely in Kirchner's work the value of detail in itself is slight, it is nevertheless important for the understanding and appreciation of his vision and the development of his method of work. A new style reveals itself not only in new proportions and dimensions but also, most particularly, in new individual forms. The coming into being of individual forms is very clearly recognizable in Kirchner's development.... Changed proportions go hand in hand with changed individual forms. The latter no less than the former are determined by the composition as a whole. But in addition to this, any particular interest which the artist takes in a form will influence the shape he gives it. Thus in a figure in which the head has a particular interest for the artist it will be rendered larger, while the other parts atrophy. Thus the proportions are graded in accordance with the feeling that gave the incentive for the work, which is thereby strongly emphasized. 'Nude Girl in Hat' is typical of this. If the forms making up this figure are compared with the natural canon all will be found distorted. Yet it is precisely these forms that bring out the thin yet still so soft woman's body. This print is worthy of a place beside Cranach's 'Venus' in Frankfurt-am-Main. Kirchner's deformations don't disturb the spectator because they are right for the picture, so that if attention is not drawn to them they will not even be noticed.

"All these means of representation are present in Kirchner's works from the beginning, but these works do not come to full development and effectiveness until he irrevocably banishes light and shade from them. Up to that point he had tried to include these in the picture by means of colour and shape. In this way he achieved a precise form. This closed form now made light and shade superfluous, for the artist recognized that he could express himself far more powerfully by means of intensification and simplification than by the use of shading and cast shadows. In this he did not seek ornamental effect but clear form-giving in terms of graphic art. He has brought this last to such a stage of dematerialization that he can make it cover everything. For him there are no themes that suit one technique rather than another. He has subjected the techniques, like the presentation, to his own needs....

"Since Kirchner does his own printing he is in a position to make full use of all technical possibilities. Only an artist with love and aptitude for handicraft ought to make prints – only if the artist does his own printing do his prints deserve the title 'original.'

"In his work Kirchner takes a naive pleasure in his materials and his techniques, and he is always discovering new possibilities, new means. The prints reveal a primal, powerful artistic sensuousness, and it is precisely the laborious graphic technique that enables this to unfold

fully. Just as the 'savage' carves the figure, the embodiment of his longing, with endless patience out of the hard wood, so does the artist form what are perhaps his purest and most powerful works in painstaking, complicated technical labour. One is reminded of the primal curse: 'By the sweat of thy brow shalt thou eat bread.'"

Etching

"Kirchner's favourite technique at present is etching, for this enables him to take his plates with him without trouble, and thus to make his first sketch direct from nature. Consequently it is the etchings, particularly in their first states, that embody the most immediate rendering. These etchings, rich as they are in temperamental 'handwriting' and various in design, are like a diary of the painter's.... The unconstrained waywardnees of this art is given full scope. Alongside these there are plates that are perfected to the last detail, worked on time after time, their originally smooth surfaces transformed by repeated bitings to a vigorous relief-map. There are plates with etched lines 2 mm wide beside others with the most delicate, gossamer-like aquatinting, spread on the polished surface with the brush, and etched patches as deep as the recesses for cloisonné enamel.... Etching is a cunning art. It is precisely the heaviest pressure in printing that produces these fine lines. They are slightly raised above the velvet-gleaming ground. The ink is pressed into the paper, thus giving an entirely different effect from lithography or woodcut, in which it only lies on top."

Prints

"The impulse that drives an artist to make prints is perhaps partly the striving to give firm and final form to the drawing with its loose, momentary quality. Moreover, the technical manipulations undoubtedly release forces in the artist which never come into their own in the far less laborious handiwork of drawing and painting. The mechanical process of printing integrates the single phases of the work into a single whole. The form-giving phase of the work can be lengthened as long as one likes without risk. There is a particular fascination in working over a plate again and again for weeks, even months, extracting the ultimate perfection of expression and form, but without sacrificing freshness. The mysterious fascination that surrounded the invention of printing in the Middle Ages can still be felt today by anybody who devotes himself seriously to print-making, right down to the mechanical details. There are no greater pleasures than those of watching the ink-roller passing for the first time over the just-completed wood-block, or etching the lithographic plate with nitric acid and gum arabic, observing whether the desired effect is making its appearance, or of tracing the maturing of the final form of a print as seen in the impressions of its states. How interesting it is to run one's finger over prints, feeling out the smallest detail, sheet after sheet, without noticing the passage of the hours. Nowhere does one get to know an artist better than in his prints."

On the "Brücke" Members
From Kirchner's diary, 1 March, 1923:
"I had shown them the technique of the woodcut, and Schmidt-Rottluff had tried his hand at lithography at an art school in Dresden, but we were only able to appreciate the value of the latter technique properly when a stone chanced to come into my possession, and after much experimenting I discovered the technical tricks for myself, as well as the process of hand-printing. When I was making my first successful print Heckel came into the studio – I can still see it – and at once recognized the great possibilities of the new technique, and soon we were all three making lithographs. Some time previously we had already had a try at etching, Heckel first, so now we had all three techniques."

EMIL NOLDE
"Nobody had ever before got the full value out of acids and the metal [in etching] in the way I did. After making the drawing on the bare copper plate and coating it more or less I laid it in the poison-bath, astonishing myself by the richness in nuances of the effects I achieved. Technique is only technique, and in itself no more than a means. Technique can be inartistic when it is brilliant."
(From "Jahre der Kämpfe," Berlin, 1934)

MAX PECHSTEIN
"The woodcut allows the least variety in technical treatment, the excitement or thoughtful calm of the cutter at any particular moment being betrayed by the trace of the knife alone. In etching one can use the various technical tricks in endless exciting ways. One can coax silvery tones with the file, can clear away the mordant with the brush, or plough the tough needle, the instrument of the will, through the metal of the plate. What a variety of effects can be achieved in the lithograph, if one prepares the stone oneself, etches and prints oneself. That is the thing – one must do one's own printing! Making the ink more or less tacky, using the paper more or less damp,

all give new charms and stimuli. What a delight when one has discovered a new craft tool oneself, and finds that it stands the test of practical work. The worker's reward is in the work itself. The effect is apparent much more promptly and more directly than in painting, and one is chained to the work until the finished print lies before one. Then one can sleep in peace. The long winter evenings suit the graphic artist, who can carry on his work by artificial light. In winter nature itself wears a more nearly black-and-white garment. In 1905, in Dresden, I made my first woodcut, using the wood-engraver's method of the tidy drawing on hard beech-wood, cut with the burin. Then I started using the gouge, which gave me greater freedom in translating my drawing, now only roughed-out, into a woodcut, and from then on I invariably used wood cut along the grain (alder, lime or poplar). Finally I took to a short cobbler's knife, letting my hand cut freely into the wood, without any drawn pattern, just as it draws with pencil on paper. In the intervals I tried my hand at lithography, which culminated in Berlin in the winter of 1908–1909. I attacked the stone with the chalk straight away, going on to apply glazes and to etch, in order to secure a lithograph that was not merely lying on the surface. Then I made the prints by hand, without a press. Fascinated, I took my stone with me to the country in summer, and toting it around I made lithographs straight from nature. At the same time I played with zinc plates, using both etching-fluid and dry-point. I applied these two methods separately until at a later time I acquired a full knowledge and a free command of technique. My basic principle, which I still hold, was that the work must be completed with the same tools with which it was begun, no pattern being made in advance on the wood, stone or metal. Sketches and drawings made previously clarify the aim, and once the idea is finished in the mind it is brought to completion by the appropriate tool."
(Quoted by Buchheim, "Die Künstlergemeinschaft 'Brücke,'" Feldafing, 1956)

MAX BECKMANN
"... All these things appear to me in black and white, like vice and virtue. Yes, black and white are my two elements. It is my good or bad fortune that I can't see everything black or everything white. A single way of looking at things would be so much simpler and clearer, but in reality it doesn't exist. Many people dream of seeing only the white and the truly beautiful, *or* only the black, ugly and destructive. But I have to take in both,

for it is only in black *and* white that I can recognize God in his unity, in his ever-repeated creation of the eternally changing drama of terrestrial things."
(From "Meine Theorie der Malerei," a lecture at the New Burlington Gallery, London, in 1938)

HAP GRIESHABER

Grieshaber is still today producing woodcuts completely in the Expressionist spirit, and he shows himself enamored of his material in much the same way as Kirchner. The following extract, which gives general information about the attitude of the artist in prints, is taken from "Rotkäppchen und der Maler" (Pfullingen, 1964).

"There was a time when my knife was poverty. There are wonderful tools for cutting wood-blocks. Burins of special steel with which wood-engravers could cut round and leave standing the finest lines in wood cut across the grain. Gouges and socket-chisels for wood cut along the grain which the Expressionists used, to let their temperament have its head. Punches and hatching-tools for fine engraving, etc. But in those days I couldn't afford such expensive tools. I worked in a machine factory, and there I ground myself a blade of spring-steel which I jammed between two pieces of wood. I still use this knife, which happens to look exactly like those used by the first cutters of wood-blocks in the Middle Ages. It serves just as well for a line-cut in the manner of the single-leaf incunabula as for a flat-colour cut with large figures. My knife always served me truly, it cut neither too coarse nor too fine but was always just suited to scoop out exactly what I wanted. The wood I cut my things in was, *faute de mieux*, simply that which came to hand: old doors, bedsteads, complete cabinets and barn-doors. Walnut is a wood for Sundays. For as long as one is working on it one is immersed in its fragrance. The grain is long and even, and cuts with precision. But unfortunately walnut was used for gun-stocks, and suddenly there was none to be had. The mould-carvers of the four-teenth century loved pear- and apple-wood. The 'Biblia Pauperum' was cut in pear-wood! Sometimes I have thought I could see the texture of Gothic drapery-folds in the layers of the grain of pear-wood. Perhaps I was lucky not to have good wood too often, but instead generally unusable beech-planks from the mountain pastures or conifer-wood from the Schwarzwald. Once an ash, blown down in a storm, fell so to speak in my lap; I lived on its iron-hard wood for a long time. (It is used for axe-handles and cartwheels.) At that time the first flat surfaces cropped up between my Gothic line-networks. From laziness, perhaps. Once one has come to terms with limitation one needs ever less. A mixture of pride and defiance, such as the miner feels when he goes down the pit, to make do with nothing round him but stone, coal, iron and wood.

"Paper was no worry. I took what I found. I printed whole block-books on filter-paper from the hospital. If the paper was too hard, then colour or extra pressure in the printing had to help out. Even packing-paper can look like old silk, if you know how. In the trade, of course, value is attached to hand-made paper, to having everything nicely in the middle, to readily-salable dimensions, and to the thing having an opulent look altogether, like a share-certificate. All the same the 'Brücke' prints, so highly-priced today, are simply on the cheapest paper the Expressionists could find in Dresden. The poor have to be on the look-out for remnants. Chance in the printing brings in many compensations there, things that set one off on fresh trails; a surprise when the print comes out of the press is always exhilarating!"

124

IX   KARL SCHMIDT-ROTTLUFF

Biographical Index

HORST ANTES
Born 1936 at Heppenheim/Bergstrasse, Germany. A pupil of Hap Grieshaber. Since 1962 has produced a wide range of engravings and lithographs. Bibliography. Günther Gercken: "Horst Antes: Catalogue of Engravings 1962–1966," Munich, 1968.

ERNST BARLACH
Born 2 January 1870 at Wedel/Holstein, Germany. 1888–1891 commercial college in Hamburg, 1891–1895 the Dresden Academy, 1895–1896 visits to Paris, Hamburg, Wedel, and Berlin, and in 1906 to Russia. 1907–1909 Berlin, 1909 Florence. In 1910 settled permanently at Güstrow/Mecklenburg, Germany. Served in World War I 1915–1916. Died at Rostock on 24 October 1938. Barlach was a writer as well as a sculptor and graphic artist. His woodcuts include a number of series, such as Goethe's "Walpurgis Nacht," "Die Wandlungen Gottes," "Der Findling," and "Der arme Vetter." Bibliography. Friedrich Schult: "E. Barlach, Das graphische Werk," Hamburg, 1958. Wolf Stubbe: "E. Barlach," Munich, 1959. Alfred Werner: "Ernst Barlach," New York, 1966.

LEONARD BASKIN
Born at New Brunswick, New Jersey, in 1922. Lives at Northampton, Massachusetts, where he has taught sculpture and graphic arts for many years. Studied in New York, Paris, and Florence. Among his artistic antecedents were Expressionists and Symbolists. His work is a large scale blend of wood engravings and woodcuts. Bibliography. Leonard Baskin: "Woodcuts and Wood Engravings: Catalogue of the Royal Watercolour Society Galleries," London, 1962.

MAX BECKMANN
Born on 12 February 1884 in Leipzig. In 1899 attended an art school in Weimar. 1903–1904 Paris. 1906 exhibited at the Berlin "Sezession." Spent some time in Florence after winning the "Villa Romana" prize. 1908 returned to Paris and joined the executive committee of the "Sezession" but withdrew in 1911. 1914–1915 served as a medical orderly in Belgium during World War I. 1915–1933 permanently in Frankfurt-am-Main, where he was appointed professor at the arts school in 1925. Between 1929 and 1932 frequent visits to Switzerland. In 1933 was deprived of his professorship in Frankfurt and banned from exhibiting. Lived in Berlin till 1937, then fled to Paris and settled in Amsterdam, where he remained till 1947. 1947–1949 on the teaching staff of Washington University, St. Louis, and in 1949 of the Brooklyn Museum in New York. Died in New York on 27 December 1950. His works, mostly pre-1923, include three hundred lithographs, engravings, and woodcuts. Bibliography. Klaus Gellwitz: "Max Beckmann, Die Druckgraphik," Karlsruhe, 1962 (catalogue Badischer Kunstverein). Curt Glaser: "Max Beckmann, Mit Oeuvre-Katalog der Graphik bis 1923," Munich, 1924. L. G. Buchheim: "Max Beckmann," Feldafing, 1959.

WERNER BERG
Born 1904 in Elberfeld, Germany. Pupil of Emil Nolde, studied in Munich and Vienna. Since 1931 has been living on a farm in Carinthia, Austria, where he has turned out a wide range of woodcuts in the style of Edvard Munch and the German Expressionists. Bibliography. Werner Berg, Woodcuts, Vienna, 1964.

GEORGES BRAQUE
Born 13 May 1882 at Argenteuil. Started as a decorator in Le Havre, but in 1900 moved to Paris to study painting. Was at first attracted by Fauvism, then turned to Cézanne. First steps in Cubism 1908. Friendship with Picasso led to studies in analytical Cubism, and in 1911–1912 of synthetic Cubism. Served in World War I 1914–1915 and was severely wounded. After a "back to Nature" period executed a number of stage designs and book illustrations. Died in Paris in 1966. Bibliography. Werner Hofmann: "Braque, Das graphische Werk," Stuttgart, 1961.

HEINRICH CAMPENDONK

Born 3 November 1889 in Krefeld, Germany. After studying with Thorn-Prikker at the School of Applied Arts in Krefeld was invited by Franz Marc to Sindelsdorf, where he met Kandinsky and August Macke and joined the "Blaue Reiter" group. After being discharged from military service, settled at Seeshaupt on Lake Starnberg, Bavaria. Appointed to the staff of the Düsseldorf Academy in 1926 and was dismissed in 1933. Accepted a new professorship at the Amsterdam Academy. Died in Amsterdam on 9 May 1957. His work consists mainly of highly decorative and ornamental woodcuts. Bibliography. M. T. Engels: "Heinrich Campendonk, Holzschnitte," Stuttgart, 1959.

CARL CRODEL

Born in Marseilles on 16 September 1894 of German parentage. After studying lithography, became an art historian in 1918. As an artist he was influenced by Munch and Kirchner. His early work consists mainly of woodcuts; later he turned to colored lithographs. Joined the staff of the Munich Academy of Fine Arts in 1951. Now lives in Munich.

ANDRÉ DERAIN

Born at Châtou, France, on 10 June 1880. 1898–1899 attended the Académie Carrière and got to know Matisse and de Vlaminck. Worked with the latter at Châtou, then in 1904 attended the Académie Julian. In 1905 worked with Matisse and contributed to the Fauves exhibition at the Salon d'Automne. From 1908 came increasingly under the influence of Cézanne and the Cubists. In 1910 worked with Picasso at Cadaquès, and in 1912 embarked on his "Gothic" period. Served in the 1914–1918 war and traveled widely between 1920 and 1930. Died on 8 September 1954. Bibliography. D. Setton: "André Derain" in the catalogue of the Exhibition of Graphic Art at the Bibliothèque Nationale, Paris, 1955.

OTTO DIX

Born on 2 December 1891 at Unterhausen near Gera, Germany. 1905–1909 studied with a Gera decorator, and 1909–1914 attended the Dresden School of Applied Art. Served in the 1914–1918 war in France, Flanders, and Russia. 1919–1922 attended the Dresden "Kunstakademie" and in 1920 contributed to the first "Dada" show in Berlin. After completing a number of paintings of World War I he embarked on a series of war engravings. 1922–

1925 at the Düsseldorf "Kunstakademie," 1925–1927 in Berlin, and in 1927 was appointed professor of monumental painting at the Dresden Academy. Was dismissed in 1933 and banned from exhibiting in 1934. Moved first to Singen and in 1936 to Hemmenhofen on Lake Constance, where he died in 1969. Bibliography. Florian Karsch: "Otto Dix, Das graphische Werk," Hanover, 1970. Fritz Löffler: "Otto Dix, Leben und Werk," Vienna, 1967.

JEAN DUBUFFET

Born in 1901 at Le Havre. Studied in Paris in 1918, but his artistic career was temporarily interrupted in 1924. In 1930 he went into business as a wholesale wine merchant, but in 1934 returned to painting, though he did not become a full-time artist till 1942. 1948–1952 exhibitions of "art brut." Lives in Paris and the south of France. Bibliography. G. Limbourg: "L'art brut de Jean Dubuffet," Paris, 1953.

CHARLES GEORGES DUFRESNE

Born on 23 November 1876 at Millemont, Seine-et-Oise, France. After studying sculpture at the Académie des Beaux Art in Paris, spent 1906 in Italy. The years 1910–1913 spent in North Africa exerted a lasting influence on his work. Died on 8 August 1938 at La Seyne-sur-mer.

RAOUL DUFY

Born on 3 June 1877 at Le Havre. In 1900 attended the École des Beaux Arts in Paris, and in 1901, like Derain, came under the influence of Van Gogh. Next came, in 1905, a "Fauviste" period under the influence of Matisse, followed by Cézanne and Cubist periods. In 1908 started working with Braque at L'Estaque. In 1909 visited Munich with Othon Friesz before turning to interior decoration. Between 1922 and 1925 paid visits to Sicily and Morocco. In 1940 he settled at Perpignan, and in 1952 at Forcalquier, where he died on 23 March 1953. Bibliography. G. Bresson: "Raoul Dufy," Paris 1953.

JAMES ENSOR

Born 13 April 1860 at Ostend, Belgium, where he settled permanently after spending 1877–1879 at the Brussels Academy. First engravings 1886. Died 19 November 1949. Bibliography. A. Croquez: "L'œuvre gravé de James Ensor," Geneva, 1947. Paul Haesaerts: "James Ensor," Brussels, 1957. Jacques Damase: "L'œuvre gravé de James Ensor," Geneva, 1967.

LYONEL FEININGER

Born 17 July 1871 in New York of German parentage. 1887–1891 at the Hamburg School of Applied Arts and the Berlin Academy. 1891–1893 studied in Paris. Until 1906 contributed caricatures to American and German publications in Berlin, and after a brief period in Paris returned in 1908 to Berlin, where he remained until 1919. During a journey to Paris in 1911 got to know Delaunay and the Cubists. In 1913 contributed to the "Blaue Reiter" exhibition in Berlin. 1919–1933 teaching at Weimar and Dessau. In 1924, along with Klee, Kandinsky, and Jawlensky founded the "Blaue Vier" group. Lived in Berlin from 1933 to 1936, and from 1937 in New York, where he died on 11 January 1956. Bibliography. Hans Hess: "Lyonel Feininger," Stuttgart, 1959. Catalogue of the Hamburg Exhibition in 1961.

CONRAD FELIXMÜLLER

Born 25 May 1897 in Dresden. Attended the Dresden "Kunstakademie" in 1912, and free-lanced from 1915. Contributed to "Aktion" 1916–1927. 1949 joined the teaching staff of the pedagogical faculty at Halle Saale University. His output includes illustrations and a number of series of engravings. Bibliography. Catalogue of the Conrad Felixmüller Exhibition at the Nierendorf Gallery, Berlin, 1965.

PAUL GAUGUIN

Born 7 June 1848 in Paris. After serving as a sailor went into business and did not take up painting until 1874. Became a friend of Pissarro's and contributed to Impressionist exhibitions. Gave up business in 1883 and in the following year visited Denmark with his family. Was divorced in 1885 and returned to Paris. In 1886 he visited Pont-Aven for the first time and so met Van Gogh. After a voyage to Martinique in 1887 met Emile Bernard in 1888 while on a visit to Pont-Aven, where he resumed acquaintance with Van Gogh. The year 1889 was divided between Pont-Aven and Paris, and in 1891 he left for Tahiti, returning in 1893. By 1895 he was back in Tahiti, and in 1900 visited the Marquesas. Died at Hiva-Hoa, Marquesas Islands, on 8 May 1903. Bibliography. M. Guerin: "L'œuvre gravé de Paul Gauguin," Paris, 1927. Libuše Sýkorová: "Paul Gauguin, Unknown Woodcuts," Prague, 1963.

VINCENT VAN GOGH

Born 30 March 1853 at Groot-Zundert, Holland. Was in business as an art dealer in Brussels, London, and Paris, but after a brief period of theological study became a lay preacher in the Belgian coal fields. First essays in painting and drawing 1880. Spent 1882–1883 in The Hague, then moved to Neunen. Studied in Antwerp in 1885, and in 1886 went to Paris, where he met Toulouse-Lautrec, Seurat, Signac, and Gauguin. In 1887 struck up a friendship with Bernard. In 1888 moved to Arles, where Gauguin came to see him. Then came his first breakdown, and in 1890 he was confined to an asylum in St. Remy. Was transferred to Dr. Gachet's clinic at Auvers in 1890 and died there on 29 July. Bibliography. J. B. de la Faille: Complete and definitive, illustrated and classified catalogue, The Hague, 1958.

HAP GRIESHABER

Born 15 February 1909 at Rot an der Rot, Upper Swabia, Germany. Has been turning out a wide range of woodcuts since 1932. Now lives at Achalm, near Reutlingen, Germany. Bibliography. Margot Feurst: "Hap Grieshaber, der Holzschneider," Stuttgart, 1964.

MARCEL GROMAIRE

Born 24 July 1892 at Noyelles-sur-Sambre, France. Self-taught, but influenced by Matisse and Cézanne. Served in 1914–1918 war and was wounded in 1916. After the war adopted a monumental version of Expressionism, largely on the advice of Léger. This versatile artist now lives in Paris. Bibliography. G. Besson: "Marcel Gromaire," Paris, (undated).

GEORGE GROSZ

Born 26 July 1893 in Berlin. Studied in Dresden (1909), Berlin (1911), and Paris (1913). Started by contributing caricatures to various satirical periodicals, then served in World War I till 1916. Settled in Berlin in 1918 and enjoyed a brief flirtation with the Dadaists before establishing contact with the "Neue Sachlichkeit" group. Between 1922 and 1928 traveled widely in Russia, France, and Switzerland. In 1932 accepted an invitation to join the teaching staff of the Art Students League in New York, where in 1933 he opened a school of his own. Returned to Germany in 1959 and died on 6 July 1959. Bibliography. H. Bittner: "George Grosz," Cologne, 1961.

ERICH HECKEL

Born 31 July 1883 at Döbeln, Saxony. In 1904 studied architecture at Dresden University of Technology, and in 1905, after meeting Kirchner, was a co-founder of the society of artists known as "Die Brücke." From 1907–

1910 divided his time between Dresden and Dangast, Oldenburg, with a journey to Rome in 1909. Moved to Berlin in 1911. Served in a medical unit in the 1914–1918 war, and in 1915 met Ensor and Beckmann. Returned to Berlin in November 1918, and after a lot of traveling settled from 1941–1943 in Carinthia, Austria, and in 1944 at Hemmenhofen on Lake Constance where he died on 27 January 1970. His works includes no fewer than 1,017 prints. Bibliography. Annemarie and Wolf-Dieter Dube: "Verzeichnis der Graphik von Erich Heckel," 2 vols., Hamburg, 1964–1965.

JOSEPH HEGENBARTH
Born 15 June 1884 at Böhmisch-Kamnitz, Bohemia. 1909–1915 studied at the Dresden Academy. Lived nearly all his life in Dresden and died there in 1961. Most of his work consists of drawings and book illustrations. Bibliography. Fritz Löffler: "Joseph Hegenbarth," Dresden, 1959.

CARL HOFER
Born 11 October 1878 in Karlsruhe and studied at the local academy. Went to Paris in 1900 and was a pupil of Hans Thoma until 1902, when he attended the Stuttgart Academy. After spending 1903–1908 in Rome he returned to Paris and stayed there until 1913, apart from travels in India in 1909 and 1911. After spending 1913 in Berlin he was interned in France during World War I. In 1918 he was appointed to the staff of the Berlin Academy. After an abstract period 1930–1931 he returned to his former style in 1932. His Berlin studio was totally destroyed in 1943 together with nearly all his works. In 1945 he was appointed head of the University of Fine Arts in Berlin, where he died on 3 April 1955. Bibliography. Catalogue of the Memorial Exhibitions in Berlin and Karlsruhe, 1956–1957.

ALFRED HRDLICKA
Born 27 February 1928 in Vienna. Sculptor, painter, and engraver. Studied painting and sculpture in Vienna from 1946–1957. Bibliography. K. Sotriffer: "Alfred Hrdlicka – Randoledtil" with a catalogue of his engravings 1947–1968, Vienna, 1969.

ALEXEI VON JAWLENSKY
Born 26 March 1864 at Kuslowo. Attended the Cadet School in Moscow, but in 1896, after a period at the St. Petersburg Academy, moved to Munich with Marianne von Werefkin to attend Anton Abbé's art school, as did Kandinsky shortly afterwards. After spending some time in Brittany during 1905 came under the influence of Cézanne, Matisse, and Van Gogh. In 1909 became a foundation member of "Neue Künstler Vereinigung" in Munich, and later established contact with the "Blaue Reiter" group. Went to Switzerland in 1914, and from 1921 settled in Wiesbaden, where he joined the "Blaue Vier" group. Died 15 March 1941 in Wiesbaden. Bibliography. Clemens Weiler: "Alexei von Jawlensky," Cologne, 1959.

ASGER JORN
Born 1914 at Vejrun, Denmark. Came to Paris in 1936 and made contact with Léger and Le Corbusier. Co-founder of the "Cobra" group in 1949. Bibliography. Ch. Dotremont: "Asger Jorn," Copenhagen, 1950.

WASSILY KANDINSKY
Born 5 December 1866 in Moscow. In his youth studied law and did not take up painting until he was thirty. In 1896 he moved to Munich where he attended Abbé's art school and studied with Franz Stuck at the Academy. In 1902 he started a school of his own and was elected president of the "Phalanx" group. He also joined the Berlin "Sezession." Between 1903 and 1907 he traveled widely in France, Tunisia, Holland, and Italy, then divided his time between Munich and Murnau, Bavaria. In 1909 he founded the "Neue Künstler Vereinigung" of Munich. In 1910 he published a book entitled "Über das Geistige in der Kunst" (The Intellectual Element in Art). Contributed to the "Blaue Reiter" exhibition in 1911, and with Franz Marc issued the "Blaue Reiter" yearbook which appeared the following year. Returned to Moscow in 1914 and joined the staff of the Moscow Academy in 1918. Moved to Berlin in 1921, and from 1922 to 1933 taught at the Bauhaus at Weimar and Dessau. In December 1933 settled at Neuilly-sur-Seine and died there on 13 December 1944. His works include some two hundred woodcuts, engravings, and lithographs. Bibliography. Will Grohmann: "Wassily Kandinsky," Cologne, 1958. Konrad Roethel: "Wassily Kandinsky, Das graphische Werk," Cologne, 1970.

ERNST LUDWIG KIRCHNER
Born 6 May 1880 at Aschaffenburg, Germany. From 1901–1905 studied architecture at Dresden University of Technology, but also found time for studying painting in Munich for two terms. Met Heckel in 1904, and a year later the two founded the artists' association "Die

Brücke" along with Fritz Bleyl and K. Schmidt-Rottluff. Spent the summers of 1907–1909 on the Moritzburg lakes near Dresden. From 1911 to 1914 was in Berlin and in touch with "Der Sturm." His period of military service brought on a mental and physical breakdown. In 1918 settled near Davos, Switzerland, and in 1923 at "Wildboden" in Sertigtal near Frauenkirch. Committed suicide at Davos on 15 June 1938. His works include no fewer than 971 woodcuts, 665 engravings, and 458 lithographs. Bibliography. A. and D. Dube: "Ernst Ludwig Kirchner, Das graphische Werk," Munich, 1967. Donald E. Gordon: "Ernst Ludwig Kirchner," together with a critical catalogue of all his paintings, Munich, 1968.

PAUL KLEE
Born 18 December 1879 at Münchenbuchsee near Bern. From 1898 to 1901 studied in Munich, and in 1901 traveled widely in Italy. From 1902–1906 was in Bern, and from 1906 in Munich, where he established cordial relations with members of the "Blaue Reiter" group. Visited Paris in 1912, and Tunisia in the spring of 1914, on the latter occasion in the company of Louis Moilliet and August Macke. From 1916–1918 served in World War I, and in 1922 was invited to join the "Bauhaus" school, as well as joining the "Blaue Vier." On the Staff of the Düsseldorf Academy from 1930–1933, but on being dismissed in 1933 moved to Bern. Died on 29 June 1940. Bibliography. E. Kornfeld: "Verzeichnis des graphischen Werks von Paul Klee," Bern, 1964. W. Grohmann: "Paul Klee," Stuttgart, 1954.

CÉSAR KLEIN
Born 1876 in Hamburg. Attended the Schools of Applied Arts in Hamburg and Berlin, and studied at the Berlin and Düsseldorf Academies. In 1919 joined the Berlin "November Gruppe." Died in 1954 at Pansdorf near Lübeck. Bibliography. Rudolf Pfefferkorn: "César Klein," Berlin, 1963.

OSKAR KOKOSCHKA
Born 1 March 1886 at Pöchlarn, Lower Austria. Attended the Vienna School of Applied Arts from 1905 to 1909 and soon came under the influence of Klimt and Van Gogh. Established contact with the "Sturm" group in Berlin, but returned to Vienna in 1911. Served in World War I 1915–1917 and was severely wounded on the Russian front. In 1917 settled in Dresden and taught at the Dresden Academy from 1920 till 1924 before embarking on extensive travels, only interrupted by a stay

in Vienna from 1931 to 1934. In 1934 left Austria for Prague, and in 1938 left Prague for London, where he acquired British nationality in 1947. Revisited Italy in 1948 and 1949, and since 1954 has been living at Villeneuve on Lake Geneva. His most important graphic works, including the lithograph portraits, were produced between 1918 and 1924. Bibliography. H. M. Wingler: "Kokoschka, das graphische Werk," Munich, 1971. H. M. Wingler: "Oskar Kokoschka, Das Werk des Malers," Salzburg, 1956.

KÄTHE KOLLWITZ
Born 8 July 1867 in Königsberg. In 1881 was given her first drawing lessons by a copper engraver, and in 1886 made a study of Max Klinger's etchings in Berlin. Back in Königsberg she turned out a number of prints between 1889 and 1891 before moving to Berlin and marrying in 1891. From 1893 her work was devoted exclusively to prints. Visited Paris in 1904 and 1907. Turned to woodcuts in 1920 on the instigation of Ernst Barlach. Died on 22 April 1945 at Moritzburg. Of her 270 separate works the majority are lithographs. Bibliography. A. Klipstein: "Käthe Kollwitz, Verzeichnis des graphischen Werkes," Bern, 1955.

ALFRED KUBIN
Born on 10 April 1877 at Leitmeritz, Bohemia. The years 1879–1883 were spent in Salzburg. He attended the School of Applied Arts there in 1891–1892 before studying photography in Klagenfurt, Austria. Further studies in Munich 1898–1901. In 1906 acquired Schloss Zwickledt near Wernstein in Upper Austria and settled there. After traveling in Bosnia and Dalmatia wrote a novel entitled "Die andere Seite." In 1909 joined the "Neue Künstler Vereinigung" in Munich and in 1912 established close relations with the "Blaue Reiter" group. Died at Zwickledt on 20 August 1959. Among his works are some 160 lithographs. Bibliography. P. Raabe: "Alfred Kubin: Leben, Werk, und Wirkung," Hamburg, 1957, with a catalogue of his graphic works.

OTTO LANGE
Born 1879 in Dresden. His most important works are his Expressionist portraits first published by Paul Westheim in his "Kunstblatt." Died in Dresden in 1944.

MICHAEL LARIONOFF
Born 22 May 1881 at Teraspol, Ukraine. After studying at the Moscow Academy paid his first visit to Paris in

1906. In 1912 issued his "Rayonistische Manifest." Settled in Paris in 1914 and designed décor for the Russian Ballet from 1915 to 1929. Died at Fontenay-aux-Roses on 10 May 1964.

WILHELM LEHMBRUCK
Born 4 January 1881 in Duisburg-Meiderich, Germany. Attended the Düsseldorf School of Applied Arts 1895–1899 and the Düsseldorf Academy 1901–1906. From 1910 to 1914 he was in Paris, and from 1914–1917 in Berlin, and from 1917–1918 in Zürich. Eventually returned to Berlin and committed suicide on 25 March 1919. Of his 200 works, 180 are etchings. Bibliography. E. Petermann: "Die Druckgraphik von Wilhelm Lehmbruck," Stuttgart, 1964.

AUGUST MACKE
Born 3 January 1887 at Meschede in Westphalia, Germany. Attended the Düsseldorf Academy from 1904–1906, and between 1905 and 1907 traveled widely in Italy, Holland, and Belgium, as well as visiting London and Paris. During the winter of 1907–1908 studied with Lovis Corinth in Berlin. Further travels in Italy and visits to Paris in 1908 and 1909. From 1909–1910 was at Tegernsee, Bavaria, where he met Franz Marc, with whom he studied at Sindelsdorf, Bavaria, in 1911. Spent 1912 in Bonn and was in touch with the "Blaue Reiter" group. After a period in Paris with Franz Marc he spent the winter of 1913–1914 near Thun, Switzerland, with the painter Louis Moilliet. In 1914 he visited Tunisia with Moilliet and Paul Klee. Was then called up and was killed on the Champagne front on 26 September 1914. Bibliography. G. Friesen: "August Macke," Stuttgart, 1957.

FRANZ MARC
Born 2 February 1880 in Munich. 1900–1903 studied at the Munich Academy, traveled in Italy in 1902, and paid an extended visit to France, returning from Paris with some Japanese woodcuts. Between 1908 and 1910 turned out most of his lithographs, mainly of animals. In 1909 moved to Sindelsdorf, Bavaria, where he met Kandinsky. Struck up a friendship with August Macke in 1910. Collaborated with Kandinsky on the 1912 "Blaue Reiter" yearbook. Visited Paris with Macke, met Delaunay, and produced his first woodcuts. Was called up in 1914 and killed at Verdun on 4 March 1916. Bibliography. Klaus Lankheit: "Franz Marc: Katalog der Werke," Cologne, 1970.

JOHN MARIN
Born in 1870 at Rutherford, New Jersey. 1889–1895 studied, and later practiced, architecture. 1899–1901 studied painting at the Pennsylvania Academy, Philadelphia, and from 1901–1903 at the Art Students League in New York. From 1905 to 1909 traveled widely in Holland, Belgium, and Italy, with an extended stay in Paris. Returned to the United States in 1911 and exhibited at the 1913 Armory Show. From then on his summers were spent in Maine and his winters at Cliffside, New Jersey. Died in 1953 at Cape Split, Maine. Bibliography. Carl Zigrosser: "The Complete Etchings of John Marin," Philadelphia, 1969.

FRANS MASEREEL
Born 1889 at Blankenberghe, Belgium. Studied for a short time at the Geneva Academy. 1909–1910 visited London and Paris and traveled in North Africa. Well known for his woodcuts, notably "My Book of Hours" and "Story without Words." Died in 1972 in Avignon. Bibliography. G. Ziller: "Frans Masereel," Dresden, 1949, with a chronological catalogue of his works.

HENRI MATISSE
Born 31 December 1869 at Le Cateau-Cambrésis, France. After studying law, took up painting in 1890. During the winter of 1891–1892 studied at the Académie Julian in Paris, and in 1893 with Gustave Moreau. 1896–1897 first essays in Impressionism. To Paris in 1899, and came under the influence of Cézanne. In 1903 he founded the "Salon d'Automne," and spent 1904 at St. Tropez. Exhibited at the 1905 Salon d'Automne exhibition as the leader of the Fauves. Traveled in 1908–1909 to Germany, 1910–1911 to Spain and Russia, and in 1911–1913 to Morocco. In 1917 settled in Nice. After spending 1943–1948 at Vence, near Nice, returned to Nice-Cimiez in 1949. Died in Nice on 4 November 1954. Bibliography. W. S. Libermann: "Henri Matisse, 50 Years of his Graphic Art," New York, 1956.

LUDWIG MEIDNER
Born 18 April 1884 at Bernstadt in Silesia. Attended the Breslau Art School 1903–1904, was a fashion designer in Berlin in 1905–1906, and studied at the Académie Julian in Paris until 1907. Returning to Berlin, he was co-founder of the "Die Pathetiker" club with Richard Janthur and Jakob Steinhardt, and in 1912 the three shared a joint exhibition. Served in World War I 1916–1918, and after the war joined the Berlin "November Gruppe."

From 1933–1937 taught draftsmanship at the Jewish School in Cologne. Fled to London in 1939 and did not return to Germany (Frankfurt/Main) until 1953. His works consist mainly of etchings, plus one or two lithographs. Died at Marxheim near Frankfurt in 1966. Bibliography. Catalogue of exhibitions in Frankfurt (art room) and at the Darmstadt Kunstverein in 1970.

WILHELM MORGNER
Born on 27 January 1891 at Soest, Germany. In 1908 studied with Georg Tappert at Worpswede, and in 1911 moved to Berlin, where he was in contact with the "Sturm," "Blaue Reiter," and "Neue Sezession" groups until 1913. Served in World War I and was killed at Langemarck on 12 August 1917. Bibliography. "Katalog des Westfälischen Kunstvereins" (Landesmuseum für Kunst und Kunstgeschichte), Münster, 1967.

OTTO MÜLLER
Born 16 October 1874 at Liebau/Silesia. Studied lithography at Görlitz from 1890–1894, and from 1894 to 1896 attended the Dresden Academy. 1896–1897 traveled in Switzerland and Italy with Gerhart Hauptmann. Spent the winter of 1898–1899 in Munich, then stayed at a number of different places in Saxony and the Riesengebirge. In 1908 moved to Berlin, in 1910 joined "Die Brücke," and in 1912 worked with Kirchner in Prague. Served in World War I 1915–1918, and from 1919–1930 was on the staff of the Breslau Academy. Died 24 September 1930 in Breslau. Bibliography. L. G. Buchheim: "Otto Müllers Leben und Werk, mit einem Katalog des graphischen Werks von F. Karsh," Feldafing, 1963.

EDVARD MUNCH
Born 12 December 1863 at Loten, Norway. A year later the family moved to Christiania (Oslo), and in 1879 he studied engineering; but from 1881–1884 he studied painting in Oslo. In 1885 he spent two weeks in Paris, and in 1888 took a house at Asgardstrand where he spent his summers. Revisited Paris from October 1889 to May 1890. The years 1891 and 1892 were divided between Paris and Nice, but from December 1892 most of his time was spent in Berlin. In 1894 came the first etchings and lithographs. Between 1895 and 1897 was back in Paris where his first woodcuts appeared in 1896. Most of the years 1900 to 1907 were spent in Germany. Suffered a nervous breakdown in 1908. From 1916 settled at Skøyen, Norway, where he died on 23 January 1944, bequeathing 1,008 paintings, 15,391 prints, and 4,443 drawings to the city of Oslo. Bibliography. G. Schiefler: "Verzeichnis des graphischen Werks Edvard Munch bis 1906," Berlin, 1907. G. Schiefler, "Edvard Munch, das graphische Werk 1906–1926," Berlin, 1928. O. Sarvik: "Edvard Munch, Graphik," Zurich-Stuttgart, 1965. W. Timm: "Edvard Munch, Graphik," Berlin-Stuttgart, 1969.

EMIL NOLDE
Born 7 August 1867 at Nolde, Schleswig, Germany. Attended the Flensburg School of Applied Arts 1884–1888, and in 1889 studied in Karlsruhe. 1892–1898 was on the staff of the St. Gallen Trade School, and in 1899 was at Dachau, Bavaria with Adolph Hoelzel. Between 1898 and 1906 visited Munich, Paris, and Copenhagen. In 1906 settled in Berlin and was a member of "Die Brücke" for a short time. In 1911 met James Ensor in Belgium, and in 1912 joined the "Blaue Reiter." 1913–1914 were spent in the Far East and among the South Sea Islands. After World War I divided his time between Berlin and Seebüll, Germany, where he died on 13 April 1956. Bibliography. G. Schiefler: "Das graphische Werk von Emil Nolde," Berlin, 1911 and 1927. Revised and expanded by Christian Mosel, Cologne, 1966.

JOSÉ CLEMENTE OROZCO
Born on 23 November 1883 at Ciudad Guzmán, Mexico. From 1908–1915 studied at the Mexico City Academy, being particularly interested in Indio and Mestizo folklore. At the outbreak of the 1913 revolution turned to political caricature and made contact with Rivera and Siqueiros. Spent 1930–1934 in the United States and Europe. Died in Mexico City in 1949. His graphic works, forty-eight in number, date from between 1928 and 1944. Bibliography. Luigi Marrozzini: "Catálogo completo de la obra gráfico de Orozco," Puerto Rico, 1970.

MAX PECHSTEIN
Born 31 December 1881 at Zwickau, Saxony. Studied at the Dresden School of Applied Arts, got to know Heckel and Kirchner in 1906, and became a member of "Die Brücke." Moved to Berlin in 1908 and was co-founder of the Berlin "Neue Sezession," 1913–1914 voyage to the Pelew Islands, 1916–1917 served in World War I, and 1919 returned to Berlin. Joined the staff of the Berlin Academy in 1923, was dismissed in 1933, and rejoined in 1945. Died on 29 June 1955. Bibliography. Paul Fechter: "Das graphische Werk Max Pechstein," Berlin, 1921.

PABLO PICASSO
Born 25 October 1881 at Málaga. After visits to Paris in 1900, 1901, and 1902 he settled there in 1904. In 1906 he met Matisse, Braque, and Kahnweiler. Took up analytical Cubism in 1909 and synthetic Cubism in 1912. His neoclassical period lasted from 1920 until 1925, when he came under the influence of the Surrealists. The famous "Guernica," with its out-and-out Expressionist elements, was completed in 1937 and preceded by a number of graphic series, including the "Dreams and Lies of Franco" etchings. The period 1947–1950 was devoted almost entirely to graphic works. He now lives in the south of France. Bibliography. Georges Bloch: "Catalogue de l'œuvre gravé et lithographie 1904–1967," Zürich, 1968.

JOSÉ GUADALUPE POSADA
Born 2 February 1851 at Aguascalientes, Mexico. Settled in Mexico City in 1887 and opened a "graphic workshop" as well as illustrating day-to-day events for a local publisher. Worked for various publications in opposition to the Diaz regime, and turned out almost fifteen thousand etchings for the publishers Arroyo alone, but only about five hundred have survived. Died in Mexico City on 20 January 1913. His work was "rediscovered" in the late 1920s. Bibliography. Armin Haab: "Mexikanische Graphik," Teufen, 1957.

ARNULF RAINER
Born 8 December 1929 at Baden, near Vienna. Since 1950 has been working in a style somewhere between fantastic visions and lunatic art, and has also experimented with working under the influence of drugs. Now lives in Vienna. Bibliography. O. Breicha: "Arnulf Rainer, Katalog des druckgraphischen Werks," Vienna, 1971.

CHRISTIAN ROHLFS
Born 22 December 1849 at Niendorf/Holstein. On the recommendation of Theodor Storm studied at the Berlin and Weimar Academies. Lost a leg in 1874. Spent most of his time in Weimar, and was introduced by Henry van der Velde to Karl Ernst Osthaus. In 1901 joined the Volkwang School at Hagen, Westphalia. Spent the summers of 1905 and 1906 at Soest, where he met Emil Nolde. Spent 1910–1912 in Munich but returned to Hagen in 1912. Domiciled at Ascona, Switzerland, in 1927. Died at Hagen on 8 January 1938. His work consists mainly of linocuts and woodcuts. Bibliography. Paul Vogt: "Christian Rohlfs, das graphische Werk," Recklinghausen, 1960.

GEORGES ROUAULT
Born 27 May 1871 in Paris. Started as a glass stainer, then studied with Gustave Moreau at the École des Beaux-Arts. Met Matisse, and in 1902 was in contact with the Fauves, taking part in the first Salon d'Automne. Took up graphic art in 1910 and from 1916–1927 worked at his "Miserere et guerre" series commissioned by Ambroise Vollard. After completing further series of illustrations he returned to painting in 1932. "Miserere et guerre" did not appear until 1948, after Vollard's death. Died on 17 February 1958 in Paris. Bibliography. Pierre Courthion: "Georges Rouault, Leben und Werk," Cologne, 1962, J. T. Soby: "Georges Rouault, Paintings and Prints," New York, 1947.

EGON SCHIELE
Born on 12 June 1890 at Tulln, Lower Austria, and studied at the Vienna Academy from 1906–1909. Was a co-founder of the "Neukunstgruppe" in Vienna in 1909. 1915–1916 served in World War I. In 1916 the art periodical "Die Aktion" produced a special issue devoted to Schiele. Died 31 October 1918 in Vienna. Bibliography. O. Kallir: "Egon Schiele, Persönlichkeit und Werk," Vienna, 1966. O. Kallir: "Egon Schiele, das druckgraphische Werk," Vienna, 1970.

DAVID ALFARO SIQUEIROS
Born 29 December 1896 at Chihuahua, Mexico. Studied painting in Mexico City from 1910–1914, then joined the revolutionary forces. Traveled in Europe from 1919 to 1922, collaborated with Rivera in Paris, and published a manifesto on how to bring about a renaissance of Mexican art. Returned to Mexico in 1922 and contributed to large-scale murals in collaboration with Orozco and Rivera. Fought in the Spanish Civil War in 1936. Has traveled widely in Europe since 1950. Bibliography. Armin Haab: "Mexikanische Graphik," Teufen, 1957.

KARL SCHMIDT-ROTTLUFF
Born 1 December 1884 at Rottluff, near Chemnitz, Saxony. In 1905 he and Heckel studied architecture at Dresden University of Technology; later he met Kirchner and became a co-founder of "Die Brücke." Lived in Dresden till 1911, then moved to Berlin. 1915–1918 served in World War I, and returned to Berlin in 1919. Visited Paris in 1924 and spent a good part of 1930 in Rome. In 1947 was appointed a professor at the Berlin Academy. Lives in Berlin. Bibliography. W. Grohmann: "Karl Schmidt-Rottluff," Stuttgart, 1956. Rosa Schapire: "Karl

136

Schmidt-Rottluff's graphisches Werk bis 1923," Berlin, 1924. Ernst Rathenau: "Das graphische Werk nach 1923," a sequel to the above, Hamburg, 1964.

RICHARD SEEWALD
Born 1889 at Arnswalde/Neimark, Germany. In 1909 to Munich to study architecture, and taught himself painting. Contributed to Expressionist exhibitions and was a member of the "Münchner Neue Sezession" and the "Berliner Freie Sezession." Now lives at Ronco, Switzerland.

JAKOB STEINHARDT
Born 21 May 1887 at Zerkow, Poland. 1906–1908 studied with Lovis Corinth in Berlin, and with Ludwig Meidner founded the "Pathetiker" group. Joined the "Sturm" group in 1912. Moved to Israel in 1933 and from 1952 was director of the Bezalel School in Jerusalem. Specialized in colored woodcuts. Died in 1968 at Nubaria, Israel. Bibliography. Leon Kolb: "The woodcuts of Jakob Steinhardt," Philadelphia, 1962.

RUFINO TAMAYO
Born 26 August 1899 at Oaxaca, Mexico. Adapted national Mexican art to contemporary trends, produced a number of murals, and was in touch with Siqueiros, Orozco, and Rivera without sharing their political convictions. Bibliography. Armin Haub: "Mexikanische Graphik," Teufen, 1957.

MAURICE DE VLAMINCK
Born 4 April 1876 in Paris. Tried a number of different ways of earning a living, and as an artist was entirely self-taught. In 1900 met Derain, with whom he formed the "Chaton" school. In 1901 Van Gogh came as a revelation, and in the same year he met Matisse. In 1905 contributed to the "Fauves" exhibition. Served in World War I and died on 11 October 1958. Bibliography. Catalogue of the S. Pollog Collection in the Bern Kunstmuseum, 1961.

BIBLIOGRAPHY

Important periodicals
Die Aktion, Edited by Franz Pfemfert, Berlin 1911–1933
Der Anbruch, J. B. Neumann, Berlin 1918–1922
Der Cicerone, Georg Biermann, Leipzig 1909–1930
Kunst und Künstler, Karl Schäffler, Berlin 1903–1933
Das Kunstblatt, Paul Westheim, Potsdam/Berlin 1910–1932
Der Sturm, Herwarth Walden, Berlin 1910–1932

On groups of artists
L.-G. Buchheim: *Die KG Brücke*, Feldafing 1956
Hans Bolliger and E. W. Kornfeld: *Ausstellung KG Brücke, Jahresmappen 1906–1912*, with a complete list of membership cards, annual reports, catalogues, etc. Bern 1958
Der Sturm: Ein Erinnerungsbuch an Herwarth Walden und die Künstler aus dem Sturmkreis. Edited by Nell Walden and Lothar Schreyer. Baden-Baden 1954
L.-G. Buchheim: *Der Blaue Reiter*, Feldafing 1959
Der Blaue Reiter, Edith by Wassily Kandinsky and Franz Marc. New documentary edition by Klaus Lankheit. Munich 1965

Il Cavaliere Azzurro: Catalogue of an exhibition in Turin in 1971

Publications quoted from (extracts)
L'art en Europe autour de 1918: Catalogue of an exhibition in Strasbourg in 1968
Aufbruch zur modernen Kunst: Catalogue of an exhibition in Munich in 1958
Hermann Bahr: *Der Expressionismus*, Munich 1916
L.-G. Buchheim: *Graphik des deutschen Expressionismus*, Feldafing 1959
Fritz Burger: *Einführung in die moderne Kunst*, Munich 1917
Kasimir Edschmid: *Über den Expressionismus in der Literatur und die neue Dichtung*, Dresden 1918
Carl Einstein: *Die Kunst des 20. Jahrhunderts*: Vol. XVI of the Propyläen Geschichte. Berlin 1926
Expressionismus: *Europäischer Expressionismus*: Catalogue of exhibitions in Munich and Paris in 1970
Fauvismus: *Der französische Fauvismus und der deutsche Frühexpressionismus*, Catalogue of exhibitions in Paris and Munich in 1966

Paul Fechter: *Der Expressionismus*, Munich 1914

O. Fischer: *Geschichte der deutschen Zeichnung und Graphik*, Munich 1951

Herbert Fürst: *The Modern Woodcut*, New York 1924

Arnold Gehlen: Zeit-Bilder. *Zur Soziologie und Ästhetik der modernen Malerei*, Frankfurt and Bonn 1960

Curt Glaser: *Die Graphik der Neuzeit*, Berlin 1922

Werner Haftmann: *Malerei im 20. Jahrhundert*, Munich 1954

Gustav F. Hartlaub: *Die neue deutsche Graphik*, Berlin 1920

Gustav F. Hartlaub: *Die Graphik des Expressionismus in Deutschland*, Stuttgart 1947

Wilhelm Hausenstein: *Barbaren und Klassiker*. Ein Buch von der Bildnerei exotischer Völker, Munich 1922

August Macke and Franz Marc: *Correspondence*, Cologne 1964

Kurt Pfister: *Deutsche Graphiker der Gegenwart*, Leipzig 1920

Posada und die mexikanische Druckgraphik 1930–1960, Catalogue of an exhibition in Nürnberg (Dürer Gesellschaft) in 1971

Hans Prinzhorn: *Bildnerei der Geisteskranken*, Berlin 1922

Wolfgang Rothe (publisher): *Der Aktivismus 1915–1920*, Munich 1969

Gustav Schiefler: *Die Inkunabeln der neuen deutschen Graphik in "Das graphische Jahrbuch,"* Darmstadt 1919

Diether Schmidt: *Künstlerschriften I and II*, Dresden 1964 and 1965

Karl Ludwig Schneider: *Zerbrochene Formen. Wort und Bild im Expressionismus*, Hamburg 1967

Kristian Sotriffer: *Printmaking; History and Technique*, New York 1968

U. Thieme and F. Becker: *Allgemeines Lexikon der bildenden Künstler*, Leipzig 1907–1950, continued by

Hans Vollmer: *Allgemeines Lexikon der bildenden Künstler des 20. Jahrhunderts*, Leipzig 1953–1962

Herwarth Walden: *Einblick in Kunst: Expressionismus, Futurismus, Kubismus*, Berlin 1917

Herwarth Walden: *Die Kunstwende*, Berlin 1918

Wilhelm Weber: *Saxa loquuntur. Steine reden. Geschichte der Lithographie*, Vol. II, from 1900 to the present day, Munich 1964

Paul Westheim: *Das Holzschnittbuch*, Potsdam 1921

Paul Westheim: *Künstlerbekenntnisse. Briefe, Tagebuchblätter, Betrachtungen heutiger Künstler*, Berlin 1925

Wilhelm Worringer: *Abstraktion und Einfühlung. Ein Beitrag zur Stilpsychologie*, Munich 1908.

INDEX

Page numbers in italics refer to the illustrations

Contents